Best Women's Monologues of 2019

Best Women's Monologues of 2019

true acting institute, editor
a smith & kraus book

A Smith and Kraus Book
177 Lyme Road, Hanover, NH 03755
editorial 603.643.6431 To Order 1.877.668.8680
www.smithandkraus.com

Best Women's Monologues of 2019 Copyright
© 2019 by Larry Silverberg
All rights reserved.

Manufactured in the United States of America

ISBN: 978-1-57525-934-5
Library of Congress Control Number: 2018915167

All monologues appearing here are by permission of playwright.

Typesetting and layout by Elizabeth E. Monteleone
Cover design by Larry Silverberg

For information about custom editions, special sales, education and corporate purchases, please contact Smith and Kraus at editor@smithandkraus.com or 603.643.6431.

TABLE OF CONTENTS

INTRODUCTION

Welcome to our new book of monologues for women, chosen for you by the team at True Acting Institute. We had thousands of submissions. The monologues that have been chosen are presented here in the book along with details about the playwright. For more information about any of the content in this book, and for production inquiries, please contact the playwright directly. Enjoy the book!

The team at True Acting Institute.
For more information about us, go to:
    www.trueactinginstitute.com

The Monologues

THE PLAY:

Woman Hollering Creek

THE PLAYWRIGHT:

Rita Anderson

SYNOPSIS:

Mary is a mysterious local who shows up at the diner. She is present but doesn't speak until she has had too much spiked punch at the Masquerade Ball, and then she spills her terrible secret. Age, race open.

ABOUT THE PLAYWRIGHT:

Rita Anderson has an MFA Creative Writing and an MA Playwriting. A published and award-winning playwright and poet, Rita went on scholarship to The O'Neill. Her play, Frantic is the Carousel, was the National Partners American Theatre (NAPAT) nominee, and Rita won the Ken Ludwig Playwriting Award, the top national prize from The Kennedy Center for "Best Body of Work." Rita has had almost 100 publications and productions, and her plays Final Conversations and Early Liberty, internationally published (www. offthewallplays.com), are on the publishers "Best Selling Plays" list. Rita also has two poetry books, The Entropy of Rocketman (Finishing Line Press) and Watched Pots: A Lovesong to Mother-hood, both of which were nominated for the Pushcart Prize. Rita is the Dramatists Guild Regional Rep (AUSTIN/SAN ANTONIO) and she's on the Social Media Team for International Center for Women Playwrights (ICWP), and she's a member of the B. Iden Payne Arts Council, but the highlight of her emerging career was sitting on a panel with Christopher Durang.

CONTACT: rita@rita-anderson.com

WEBSITE: www.rita-anderson.com

The Monologue:

Mary:

You oughta not talk to me, Hannah. *(hiccup)* —I'm a murderer. Yes, a murderer. Do you recall a terrible accident out on Farmer's Market Road? Happened this time of year. Fall. On a sunny Tuesday, not like you'd expect. I was late getting Brandon, that's my son, to the dentist. Speed limit said 35. I was doing 50. Accidents happen, sure. But I was rushing or I would've seen the 18-wheeler. And, because I was late, I didn't fuss at Brandon for taking off his seat belt to get one of his "guys" in the back seat. —That's what he called them, his "guys," but it was like a Power Ranger, a toy. It was blue and you could bend him into different positions. —When the truck hit us, it sideswiped a bus that was going to the zoo. Brandon landed in Woman Hollering Creek. Might have survived—if the creek bed wasn't dry. But it always is this time of year. Part of me died with him. Most of me really. *(laughs)* "Woman Hollering Creek," can you imagine!

THE PLAY:

Blackbirds' Garden

THE PLAYWRIGHT:

Merlaine Angwall

SYNOPSIS:

It is Christmas, 1844. Eliza Farnham, Matron of Mount Pleasant Prison confronts Bessie, a difficult and belligerent inmate concerning what she would do if she had money and freedom. Farnham was ahead of her time, creating sweeping prison reforms, treating prisoners humanely and fairly.

ABOUT THE PLAYWRIGHT:

Merlaine Angwall's play, Blackbird's Garden, won the international Gloria Ann Barnell Peter Playwright Competition. Blackbird's Garden was performed at UW Oshkosh, Theatre Z, and the Morgan Opera House, Aurora, NY.

Merlaine currently teaches acting, directing, musical theatre and movement at the University Wisconsin Oshkosh. Merlaine works professionally as an actor in stage, film, and television, having previously performed with several theatre companies including First Stage Milwaukee, Toledo Repertory Theatre, and The Dallas Theatre Center. She performed with the Broadway cast of *Lombardi* at the Fox Cities Performing Arts Center, and at Lambeau Field in Green Bay. Merlaine is also a director and has directed for numerous theatre companies such as the Dallas Theatre Center, New American Theatre, The Tulsa Opera and the U.S. Naval Academy. Merlaine directed the premier of That's Entertainment with the Tulsa Symphony, was an Artist in Residence for the state of Oklahoma and wrote the musical score for *Alice in Wonderland or Not!*, which premiered at the University of Colorado. She holds an M.F.A. from Trinity University.

CONTACT: Merlaine Angwall, (920) 279 – 0990

angwall@uwosh.edu

THE MONOLOGUE:

Eliza:

How? How could gold help you? Yes, gold can help you buy things, keep you from starving. But once you've fed yourself, then what? Now, you have a way out of your old life. If you want it. It takes time and patience. You read and write well. You can get a job and support yourself. You have skills. Money will buy you things, but knowledge is the real key to freedom. The knowledge, all of you gain here, is only a start. From here, all of you will grow. Teach your children and, through education, they will find their own way out of darkness. A way out of the life you lived.

(She crosses to Bessie)

Here, take my keys.

(All are astounded. Bessie stares at the keys.)

Take them. Think of it as a Christmas present.

(The Captain takes a step in – watching Bessie. Bessie slowly reaches for the keys, and holds them in her hand.)

You'll be out of here. But where will you go? Back to Five Points? Back to your old life? That's all in the past.

(Bessie starts to leave, she gets as far as the door where the captain stands.)

Will you ever see your boy Danny? What if I could bring Danny here to you?

(This stops her in her track, she turns and faces Eliza)

You can both learn together and find your own real freedom. You want a way out? I know the way. Siempre Adelante! Always Forward! And don't look back.

(Eliza crosses back to her chair. Pause. Bessie drops the keys where she stands and Captain picks them up and exits. Bessie crosses back to her chair).

THE PLAY:

Guten Morgen!

THE PLAYWRIGHT:

Cynthia Faith Arsenault

SYNOPSIS:

An elderly Holocaust survivor still dreams of her idyllic childhood in stark contrast to her nightmare in later years in the camp.

ABOUT THE PLAYWRIGHT:

Cynthia Faith Arsenault, psychologist by day, writer by night, is a former director, whose playwriting group, aptly named Group, encouraged her to take up the pen. Five years later, she is published in "Best of 5 Minute Plays for Teens," "Best 10 Minute Plays of 2017," "A Solitary Voice," and multiple times at Monologuebank,com. There have been over 80 productions of her short plays at such Boston area venues the Firehouse and Boston Playwrights Theatre; Cohasset Drama; Hovey; Our Voices; Acme; Image; Company Theatre; Acton 3, and The Actors Studio of Newburyport—as well as in most other states, and Canada, London and Australia.

CONTACT: cynthiafaith@comcast.net

WEBSITE: https://newplayexchange.org/users/2521/cynthia-faith-arsenault

THE MONOLOGUE:

(An elderly Jewish woman, sitting in a chair, has dozed off. She is suddenly wakened from a deep sleep, and tries to orient, as she addresses the facility nursing assistant.)

(Startling) Ach, you scared me! I was… it was … I was in a dream. So real …Yah, nu?… Awake, but not really — and wanting to stay —in the dream… Yah? Maybe shut my eyes… for a bit… a bit more… a minute… it was so… I was so…

(Resigned) Oh, All right…

What? The dream?

Yah, ok ... since you ask, ok... I was six... no, seven... Six, seven. And just like in real life, Mama is waking me like every morning, every day the same way, gently shaking and singing in her sweet voice:

(Singsong) "Guten Morgen!" And every day I would hear :

"Today has much promise. What a day we shall have!"

So I'd shake the sleep out of my eyes, as she'd sit on my bed, braiding my long hair, talking about the day to come. About our chores, though they weren't so much chores to me, so maybe not the best word. I learned how to keep a kosher house, an orderly house: Wash our sheets in the tub in the yard; hang them with pins on the clothesline; pare and put golden potatoes on the boil into the heavy pot that was her mother's; and set the table for dinner - two forks, sharp knife, gleaming spoon. Every morning, as we worked side by side, she'd tell me she was proud of me, that I was a smart girl, that I would do well in the world. That made me glow inside. And then, if we had time before school, we'd run up the hill, gathering wildflowers. Sometimes we'd lie on the sweet-smelling grass, watching clouds, shaped like elephants or cats, which melted into the bluest blueness. Then we'd race back to the house, and she'd let me win. Just now... I was running down the hill. Just now... before I woke up...I turned and saw her behind me, laughing. Ahh.....yah.

Much later I'd look forward to the nighttime, shut my eyes, and be back there with mama—

until morning, when I would hear "Guten Morgen!"— but now in a woman's harsh and ironic voice, followed by: " Die Gräben werden nicht selbst zu graben!"

(Yanked from her thoughts, she repeats the nurse's question) "What's that mean?"

(Pause) "Those ditches aren't going to dig themselves!"

And I'd start a different day with no promise.

THE PLAY:

A Rum Cake for Rita

THE PLAYWRIGHT:

David-Matthew Barnes

SYNOPSIS:

Marla, who is in her late 20's, explains to her sister-in-law, Rita, why her family is having a hard time dealing with the death of their son, John, who was also Rita's husband.

ABOUT THE PLAYWRIGHT:

David-Matthew Barnes is a bestselling author, playwright, poet, and screenwriter. To date, he has written over fifty stage plays that have been performed in three languages in ten countries. His literary work has appeared in over one hundred publications. He is a member of the Dramatists Guild of America, International Thriller Writers, and the Society of Children's Book Writers and Illustrators. He earned an MFA in Creative Writing at Queens University of Charlotte in North Carolina. Having lived around the world, he calls Chicago his hometown.

CONTACT: Blue Dasher Press at bluedasherpress@gmail.com

WEBSITE: davidmatthewbarnes.com

THE MONOLOGUE:

Marla:

It's Christmas Eve. This isn't easy for me. My folks are good people. They'll come around. I know they will. They're old fashioned. They're set in their ways. They just need some time. I feared this. That you would be so sad. I don't want you to be sad, Rita. You lost a husband and I lost a brother. The pain runs deep in my world, too. My mother couldn't bear it. She's a broken woman because of what happened to John. She spends most of her days and nights locked in her bedroom and I have to stand by and watch it happen. John was the lucky one in our family. He had the looks and the brains and the ambition to get out of our neighborhood. He gave us a beautiful sense of pride. Through him, we had hope our mother wouldn't have to work so hard and our father would be a kinder man. We dreamed because of him. We knew that someday, the world would be a better place because of him. We believed in John. He made us feel alive. I'm here tonight because this is where my brother's spirit is. *(Beat.)* Maybe I wanted to be close to him on Christmas Eve, to spend some time with him. *(Beat.)* To see the world again, through his eyes. It would be easier to blame all of this on Vietnam. Personally, I'm tired of all the fighting. *(Beat.)* It doesn't make sense to me. I never gave it much thought, Rita. What it means to be somebody's sister-in-law. *(Beat.)* I'm sorry.

And now, another monologue from David-Matthew Barnes.

THE PLAY:

Fractured

SYNOPSIS:

Wendy is a twenty-year-old college student who teeters on the edge of sanity. After Anthony, the object of her intense crush, reveals he's transferring to another school in the morning, Wendy responds.

THE MONOLOGUE:

Wendy:

What do you want from me? Just tell me. *(Suddenly:)* I don't want you to leave. I know I say hateful things, but I will die here without you. Don't leave me, Anthony. I beg you. If I ever meant anything to you – I've listened to you for two years. And I believed that you cared and that we would be together. *(A challenge:)* I'll kill myself. Over you. Because of you. It will hang over you like your father's death. You make me so desperate. You only have to breathe. Just stay with me, Anthony. Just for tonight. You can leave in the morning. It was so beautiful. That night. We went to the movies and it was a love story. They were friends and they realized that they were in love. I cried. Do you remember? And after the movie, we went out to that restaurant on Belmont and we ate slices of apple pie and drank hot chocolate and we talked about philosophy and religion and when we thought the world was going to end. And when we left that restaurant, it was raining. It was September and the city glowed on the asphalt. And we shared an umbrella and you held my hand and you walked me home. And Chicago seemed so sacred to me. I was so glad to be here and to be alive. I felt free. And I invited you in and…I will always have this memory of you. You inspire me. I just want you to know that. I'll write a poem about you. I'm working on it now. Here. In my head. *(After a moment:)* I don't ever want to see you again.

The Play:

Icebox Placenta

The Playwright:

Melissa Bell

Synopsis:

Patti wants to follow a holistic ritual for her child's birth placenta, but finds it challenging in the middle of the city; and so, keeps it in her freezer for four years.

About The Playwright:

Melissa Bell creates new works for the stage that evoke themes found in classical literature, featuring strong roles for women. Full length plays include COURAGE, featuring Debra Winger, produced by NACL Theatre; DEVIL & THE DEEP, music by Graham Russell of Air Supply and Katie McGhie, produced Off-Broadway by Theatre East. Staged readings: LADY CAPULET, a Henley Rose Playwright Competition for Women Finalist 2017, produced by Turn To Flesh Productions 5th Annual Staged Reading; LOST IN LOVE, a one-night only benefit for The Actors Fund produced by the Triad Theatre, featured Constantine Maroulis, Andrea McArdle, and Graham Russell, who wrote the score. LOVE, SEX, ANARCHY received a JDT-Lab at East Hampton's Guild Hall and had readings at Corner Arts Center and National Museum of Women in the Arts in DC. Short works include: GAME BOY at Future Is Female Festival, ANGEL OF HOPE at The Bechdel Group and Marble Summer Arts Festival, MINI'S COMEBACK at Feisty Female Festival, ICEBOX PLACENTA at Reproductive Freedom Festival and Mother-Lode Festival. Columbia University, BA. WriteNow Workshop and 29th Street Playwrights Collective Resident Playwright. Plays available on New Play Exchange.

Contact: TheMelissaBell@live.com, 917-940-9811

Website: https://newplayexchange.org/users/4491/melissa-bell

http://www.29thstreetplaywrightscollective.org/melissa-bell.html

THE MONOLOGUE:

Patti:

(Opens her freezer door and gazes into it.)

I would have so much more room in my freezer if it wasn't filled with placenta. No, it's not a natural hair conditioner. Real placenta. They don't let you take home your placenta if you have a hospital birth. They consider it a bio-hazard, as if something from my vagina could blow up the world. But I had a home birth, and mid-wife got me into this idea of doing something with my placenta. I want to bury it. Some cultures do that. It has something to do with nourishing the earth, putting life back into the ground. Then they plant a tree over it. But it's tough to find a place on West 43rd Street in New York City where you can plant a tree, let alone bury a placenta. But then there's this community garden on W48th Street, the one between Ninth and Tenth. I wanted to bury it there, but I don't have a plot. So I asked this gay couple: 'Can I bury my son's placenta in your plot?' They gave me a look and said "No." Some cultures bury the boy's placenta under the threshold, and the girl's under the cornerstone… or is it the girl's under the threshold? Well… I can't remember which goes where, but you can't do that when you live in an apartment building. I think you're supposed to bury it in the place where they were born ... or maybe it's the place where you want them to end up. You wouldn't want to get that wrong. Can you imagine Jake saying 'I can't get out of the stock market because my mother buried my placenta on Wall Street.' Talk about a controlling mother…Then I was thinking of putting it in the Hudson River…you know, water, the giver of all life, but… naahh… In some cultures, they eat it or make broth of it. For the protein. I mean it looks like any other slab of meat. My husband's a chef, so I said, maybe stir-fry with onions and a little truffle? He said no way. Besides, we're vegans. But does eating a part of one's own body count as eating an animal? Or would it make me a cannibal? I didn't kill it, I created it, so what's wrong with eating it? Now I'm reading that someone will take it and turn it into placenta pills—to fight off post-partum depression. My husband wants me to throw it out, but I can't. So here it is four years later, taking up all the room in my freezer. I really want to do something with it. Is there an expiration date?

THE PLAY:

Garbage Person Karaoke

THE PLAYWRIGHT:

Caroline Bennett

SYNOPSIS:

Grace just got out of an abusive relationship and is about to foray into the world of online dating. This is ill-advised.

ABOUT THE PLAYWRIGHT:

Caroline Bennett is a New York City-based playwright whose one-act comedy Garbage Person Karaoke appeared at Manhattan Repertory Theatre and the Capital Fringe Festival in Washington, DC. Her second show, Devices of Torture, premiered at the 2018 New York International Fringe Festival (FringeNYC) and was named a "Best Bet" by the review website Theater is Easy.

CONTACT: caroline.k.bennett@gmail.com, 202-725-1051

WEBSITE: carewrites.co

THE MONOLOGUE:

Grace:

When you are single, when you become single abruptly, you will find that you suddenly have a lot of time. Nothing but time, in fact.

Just reams, and reams of it.

There are a lot of things you can do with time.

You can drink, for instance!

Oh gosh.

You can do SO MUCH drinking.

So much.

And in such a short amount of time.

But the thing about drinking is its immediate after-effects. They stretch out like fingers and mess up how you see your whole life.

And so, in not a lot of time, you're doing one of two things. You're yelling at the painting on your wall. Or you're crying because the painting isn't yelling back.

There are other things you can do with time too!

Like have sex with random strangers.

Want to make sure you never see them again? Do it on your period and don't tell them! Ha HA! I mean hey! You won't get pregnant, right? And you can just clean your sheets later.

I have never done this.

But do you know what happens the next morning?

When both of you are lying in bed and sunlight is SCREAMING at you to wake up?

You get up. And he gets in a car. And you still have so. Much. Time.

A lot of time to hear yourself think. And hear what you would like to do. What you would like to see. Who you would like to spend time with.

And you can do it without that dread that somewhere, he is growling under his breath at you, and planning his next storm when you come home.

You have so much time to rebuild now.

That storm is over.

(Long beat.)

You also have time to try online dating!

You should do it!

Am I actually ready to do it? Nope! Deeeefinitely not!

But my friends somehow match up on these things all the time. And all these dumb apps are free to download! So why not have a tragic adventure with a person whose name you'll forget?

Try Bumble!

Do Bop It!

Get on Queefstr!

Eat Coffee Meets Bagel!

Try Chocolate Milk on a Hot Day!

Test out Fuckstk!

That one is like the word Fuckstick but most of the second syllable is missing. So it's pronounced "Fuxtk." The kids know what they're doing on that one. If-yuh-know-what-I-meeeean huh huh huh am I right am I right oh god kill me!

(Beat.)

This all sounds impossibly exhausting.

But people are afraid to let wounds seep and heal after they get stabbed.

By people, I mean me.

So excuse me as I judge others while doing exactly the thing I'm judging them for.

(Pulls out phone)

Hello, Fuck Stick!

Person Number One!

I am a man posing with a tiger nestled close to my bosom, about to breastfeed it. My face is one of pensive compassion, but also fear that this tiger might bite off my nipple, and perhaps even kill me and feed me to his tiger friends. This photo shows that I am tender with animals, but also have a daring *(some might say insane or stupid)* sense of adventure.

Swipe right or left?

Oookay. Person Number Two.

I am a man posing sternly in my computer room or study. All you can see is my head. My hair is long and tied back low *(it is like a man bun but I will get very offended if you call it a man bun)*. Some scraggly hairs are sticking out of my face in different directions. They look like pubic hair.

(She swipes accordingly.)

Person Number Three!

I am a sort of attractive man in a candid photo taken while performing on a stage somewhere with a guitar! In my next photo, I am making a face wearing a silly hat at a party! In my third photo, there are 40 people all standing together and smiling, and it's impossible to tell which one is me. And in my last photo, I'm standing in my bathroom and I don't have a shirt. Or a head! Swipe right or left?

(She swipes accordingly.)

And lastly, Person Number Four.

I am not a photo of a man. My picture is a woman's shadowy profile with a man's hand around her neck! My next photo is a similar but different woman's side profile with a man's hand on her forehead. Like he's petting a dog! The third photo is two naked people holding each other in a bed.

There's a word next to them in all caps that just says *(waves hands for emphasis)* "THIS."

(Beat.)

My profile reads "Looking for someone to dominate, explore, and love. None of these photos are actually of me. If you're interested in adventure, just swipe right. I don't bite. Hard." Wink! Followed by thirty emojis.

How would straight men react if a woman made this exact same profile, with the genders flipped? If it was a woman's hand on a man's neck or forehead, and that same "THIS" cuddling, and that same blurb about biting and adventure and emojis?

Would they still be up for an "adventurous lifestyle" after they had sex and came seven or eight times, and had that fantasy dissolve into real life like it always does?

Or would they grab their stuff and run as soon as it wasn't comfortable or sexy anymore?

(Beat.)

This has been "Deep Thoughts on Fuck Stick."

(She bows.)

Fuck.. I'm so tired.

The Play:

Whale Song

The Playwright:

Chantal Bilodeau

Synopsis:

Whale Song tries to make sense of the wreckage caused by Harvey the hurricane and Harvey the Hollywood producer, both of whom made the news in 2017. In the play, a woman running from her abusive husband crashes a scientific conference to ask attendees for their help in fighting all the Harveys of this world.

About The Playwright:

Chantal Bilodeau is a playwright and the Artistic Director of The Arctic Cycle, an organization that uses theatre to foster dialogue about our global climate crisis, create an empowering vision of the future, and inspire people to take action. She is currently writing a series eight plays that look at the social and environmental changes taking place in the eight Arctic states, runs the online platform Artists & Climate Change, and is a co-organizer of Climate Change Theatre Action – a worldwide series of readings and performances of short climate change plays presented to coincide with the United Nations COP meetings.

Contact: chantal1402@me.com

Website: cbilodeau.com

The Monologue:

A Woman:

Harveys are very clever. By the time you realize what they're up to, it's too late and your only option is to get out. Or, as I like to call it, to migrate. Which means to go from one place to another. Or to empower yourself by adapting to changing circumstances rather than being victimized by them. The opposite is to remain.

Do not remain. Under any circumstances. Because you can't fight a Harvey. Look at what happened in Texas. Look at what happened in Hollywood. Look at what happened to me.

Pause.

Animals migrate too. They migrate for food, better climate, to escape predators, or birth their young. Whales in particular are expert migrators. These big mamas kick ass, excuse my language. I mean, you gotta hand it to them – they can evolve quicker than you can say hyppytyynytyydytys. *(to audience)* Isn't that the craziest Finnish word? I don't even know if it's real – I found it on the Internet. Say it with me: hyppytyynytyydytys. ... It means: "Bouncy cushion satisfaction." *(laughs)* I mean, how do you put that in a sentence? "Honey, today while you were at work, I experienced bouncy cushion satisfaction." Or "Thank you so much for having us over! Your couch has such good hyppytyynytyydytys."

Pause.

Whales used to be land animals. 50 million years ago, they had four legs and huge teeth. Then the ice sheets melted, the oceans rose, and when it became clear there wasn't gonna be enough land for everyone, the big mamas were like: "We're outta here." And they migrated to the ocean. How's that for a winning strategy? "Shrink those legs and grow some fins, bitches! We're diving in!"

(to an audience member.) Have you ever heard a whale sing? ... It's amazing, right? *(or "It's really amazing" if the answer is no.)* Listen.

She plays a whale song on her phone.

I wish I spoke Whale... Or is it Whalish, like Finnish? Or Cetaceanese? ... I'd ask them: "How did you know?" Because, think about the people in Texas who didn't leave until the water was up to their second floor. Think about the women in Hollywood who didn't walk out of that hotel room until he had gotten his way. Think about me and Teri and Allison and all the beautiful wonderful women out there who have found themselves in the same situation. Why didn't we know? Why didn't we migrate before it was too late? Is there something wrong with us?

The whale song ends.

Whales are smart. They didn't wait until it was too late. And some of that migrating was tricky: they had to move their nose up to the top of their head, develop a communication technology that would work under water, and grow baleen for filtering food.

Me? Nothing that elaborate. I'm still trying to grow a thick skin so I have a long way to go.

THE PLAY:

Alabaster

THE PLAYWRIGHT:

Audrey Cefaly

SYNOPSIS:

June, a reclusive folk artist, tells the story of when her small Alabama farm was destroyed by a tornado. She lost her entire family in the tragedy, including her father, mother, and baby sister Amy.

ABOUT THE PLAYWRIGHT:

Cefaly is a southern writer and Alabama native. Her plays include The Gulf (Edgerton Award, Lammy Award, Samuel French OOB Fest Winner, Charles MacArthur Award Nominee); Alabaster (NNPN Showcase, David Calicchio Prize); Maytag Virgin (Womens Voices Theater Festival); The Last Wide Open; Love is a Blue Tick Hound, and The Story of Walter. Cefaly has developed plays with Signature Theatre, Serenbe Playhouse, Aurora Theatre, Florida Rep, Theater Alliance, Quotidian Theatre Company and Contemporary American Theater Festival. She is published by Samuel French, Smith & Kraus (two volumes of Best American Short Plays), and Applause Books. Cefaly was recently named a Traveling Master by the Dramatist Guild Foundation.

CONTACT: alcefaly@gmail.com, 301-502-0827

WEBSITE: audreycefaly.com

THE MONOLOGUE:

June:

Mama was up late doin laundry, same as always, just got home from a double at the hospital and she was so tired, so I went and fed Amy and put her down in her crib.

She wanted me to sing to her. I remember her smilin through the bars at me, blinkin those pretty eyes, like I'm not sleepy, but she was fightin. I said little girl, you will not win, I will sing you down and you will not win. She fought so hard. But she finally fell asleep with her little rag doll and I passed out in the rocker.

It came in the night. It was so...weird...I woke up thinkin has mama turned on the attic fan, all the air was movin from the room and Amy yellin "train, it's a train, Jubee!" I looked up and the window was gone, like fuckin gone. And then it was black. Everything was black. I could hear mama callin from the porch. And little Amy was screamin her head off, "Jubee, Jubee," reachin for me. I snatched her up, ran to the porch, and mama yellin get in the cellar. I ran around to the side yard and grabbed ahold of the cellar door and it ripped away from me, right outta my hands, right off the hinges, knocked me back. Holdin on to Amy so tight, and mama screamin "where's daddy?" It was all I could do to hold onto Amy, she was...she was so scared, she was callin for the cat, "Where's Pekoe? Where's Pekoe?"

And the rain, god the rain, and the noise, I couldn't hear a thing. I looked up to see a flash of white headed into the barn, maybe a hundred yards, but I knew it was daddy, seein about the horses. I called to him...

And then it came. And it was around us. The most sickening sound I have ever heard, and it was like God had reached down and twisted off a piece of the earth.

And then nothin... for like... whole seconds. It was the barn. With daddy in it. And it was gone. It was there and then it was gone. I couldn't get into the cellar... there was nothin to grab hold of. And then the porch broke sideways, right offa the house, and Amy still hollerin for Pekoe and mama screamin, "The porch, the porch!"

You try to tell people what it feels like...when a barn and half a house rains down on top of you. It's not a storm. It's not an accident. It's 3.2 seconds and it's a thousand rusty knives before you have time to pray, and then it's pushin you down into the cold red mud and the world is gone and I'm dead, this is it.

But that wasn't even the worst part. Layin there in the dark and this sound...this awful sound...so loud, and it's over and over, and its not stoppin, like a hammer, and it's louder and louder.

And it's findin out it's my own chest and whatever's left inside tryin to chew its way out with its teeth. And then Amy's sweet little voice...so soft and still, like she was talkin in her sleep...and she was so far away—how did she get so far away...

"Where's Pekoe? Where's Pekoe?"

All gone...

THE PLAY:

Angled Light

THE PLAYWRIGHT:

Andrea Fleck Clardy

SYNOPSIS:

Kate doesn't like her stepfather's politics and Kate's mother doesn't like Kate's wife. But a startling experience one bright spring morning inspires Kate to reach out to her mother.

ABOUT THE PLAYWRIGHT:

Andrea Fleck Clardy is a Boston playwright and activist, who worked in small press publishing for thirty years. Her short plays and monologues have been widely produced. Full lengths include *Hide and Seek* with music and lyrics by Clark Gesner, the creator of *You're a Good Man, Charlie Brown*, which premiered at the Hangar Theatre; and *Job Loss Figures*, winner of the Promising Playwright Award, which premiered at Colonial Players in Annapolis MD. She is a proud member of Dramatists Guild and the National Writers Union. Many of her plays are available on the New Play Exchange.

CONTACT: afleckclardy@gmail.com, (617) 435-1521

WEBSITE: andreafleckclardy.com

THE MONOLOGUE:

Kate:

(Attractive woman in her forties, wearing running clothes. She has ear buds and a phone in her hand. She dials, listens before she speaks.)

Mom, it's Kate. Are you there and just not picking up? Please take my call if you're there. I've got a great story to tell you.

Well, I guess I'll tell your voicemail the story. Then you won't be left wondering why I called after however long it's been.

This morning was amazing. Everything looked bright and clean and I went out early enough that the light was angled, still a little pink from the sunrise. It was striking the trees around the pond from just above the horizon.

When I walk, I try to be in the moment. That's the kind of statement that drives you crazy. I know. I just mean that I try to let go of my mental lists: the things I have to do, the stupid mistakes I've made. I try to keep my mind quiet and notice what I'm seeing along the way.

When I finished my walk, I crossed the street from the pond. I was heading through town. Then I looked up and there you were, walking right towards me. You looked great! Was that a little smile on your face? Were you glad to see me? My heart leapt. I tried to figure out what you were doing in my neighborhood. You must be coming to find me!

I picked up the pace, walking faster, then running towards you. You moved towards me and, in that rush, that shared eagerness, I saw the truth. I was running toward my reflection in the open door of the Centre Street Café.

When I stopped, my heart pounded. It wasn't the few yards of running. It wasn't the cliché of seeing myself as you. It was delight that pumped my heart, delight at the illusion that you had sought me out and were hurrying to hold me in your arms.

We're a lot alike, Mom, quite apart from the dark eyes and the long stride. I'm as stubborn as you are. But what the angled light showed me is how much I miss you. Look, I don't expect I'll ever think of Tom as my father. But if you're happy, I can learn to get along with him. I don't expect you to welcome Jasmine as my wife. But fair is fair. We both know that. If I can put my politics and all the rest of it aside for you, maybe you can put a little of your religion or whatever it is aside for me.

One way or another, let's get together. Please. Give me a call and we'll figure something out. I love you. See you soon.

THE PLAY:

The Burn

THE PLAYWRIGHT:

Philip Dawkins

SYNOPSIS:

Tara, black, wealthy female, high school senior forced to be in a production of The Crucible at her school, suddenly makes a realization about the title

ABOUT THE PLAYWRIGHT:

Philip Dawkins is a Chicago/Montréal playwright and educator whose plays have been performed all over the world. His plays include Failure: A Love Story (Victory Gardens Theater), Le Switch (About Face Theatre, The Jungle), The Homosexuals (About Face Theater), The Burn (Steppenwolf for Young Audiences), Dr.Seuss's The Sneetches, the Musical with composer David Mallamud (Children's Theater Company, Minneapolis) and The Gentleman Caller (Raven Theatre, Chicago; Abingdon Theatre, NY). He received the Joseph Jefferson Award for Best New Work for his plays Charm (Northlight Theatre; MCC) and Miss Marx: Or The Involuntary Side Effect of Living (Strawdog Theatre), as well as the Joseph Jefferson Award for Best Solo Performance for his play, The Happiest Place on Earth (Sideshow Theatre/Greenhouse Theater Center). Philip has been a fellow at the Hawthornden Castle International Retreat for Writers in Scotland and the MacDowell Colony in New Hampshire. Philip often teaches playwriting at his alma mater, Loyola University, Chicago. Many of his plays, including his scripts for young performers, are available through Dramatists Play Service, Playscripts, Inc. and Dramatic Publishing. He is currently working on a commission from Children's Theater Company and an American English translation of Michel Tremblay's Messe Solennelle Pour Une Pleine Lune D'été for Sideshow Theatre. Against all his better judgment, Philip has been known to perform with the French/English bilingual improv group, Frogprov.

CONTACT: philipdawkins@gmail.com

AGENT: Beth Blickers, APA, PH: (212) 621-3098

THE MONOLOGUE:

Tara:

Oh my god, oh my god, wait, no, I get it! I totally get it, because—okay, because, like, in olden times? Like back in the Pilgrims and Pocahontas and whatever—- like in the time of The Crucible—everybody was all about being terrified of witches, right? Like, if something bad happened to you, like your kid got measles or your pumpkin crop died or whatever, you'd be like, "Oh shit, it's witches." So if you just didn't like somebody, like say they overcharged you for—I don't know—a bowl of acorn soup or something, you could just accuse them of being a witch, and then like, that was it. Boom, Witch! Busted. And since everyone in America at that time was like basically a religious fascist, they thought the best way to test if you were a witch or not was to full-on set you on fire. Cuz, supposedly, if you didn't burn, that meant you were a witch, and then I guess they were like, "Great, she's a witch. Now what?" But, if you did burn—and this is where it gets like all kinds of crazy water-boarding mentality—if you did burn, then they'd be all "Oh, guess she was just a regular old human after all. Sorry not sorry." And it's like, of course they all burned, because, PS, there's no such thing as witches, A-holes. So, it's like, yeah, congratulations or whatever, you discovered who she really is; you also killed her.

THE PLAY:

The Spare Change of Strange Angels

THE PLAYWRIGHT:

Cayenne Douglass

SYNOPSIS:

Melissa Town, a prominent lawyer gets stranded on her way to a conference and ends up having an interaction with Bush, a homeless woman in downtown Los Angeles. Through a conversation they find they have something in common which alters their preconceived beliefs about their shared but separate traumatic experience. In the immediate moment prior to this monologue Melissa Town asks Bush if she has a child.

ABOUT THE PLAYWRIGHT:

Cayenne Douglass's plays have been produced at New Perspectives Theatre Company, Dixon Place, Midtown International Theatre Festival, The Big Apple Theatre Festival, ESPA Primary Stages Detention Series, Manhattan Repertory Theatre, The Players Theatre, FEAST: A Performance Series, The Village Playwrights, The Living Room Theatre, Step 1 Theatre Project, CalArts New Work Festival, Edmunds Driftwood Players in Seattle and "Ain't I a Woman" in Louisville, KY. In 2018, Cayenne participated in The First Stage Residency through The Drama League and was awarded The Barn Arts Residency in Bass Harbor, ME and The Emerging Artists Residency [in association with the Jerome Foundation] at The Tofte Lake Center in Ely, MN. She has previously been published by Smith & Kraus in The Best Men's Stage Monologues 2018 and The Best Women's Stage Monologues 2018. Cayenne attended CalArts in the theater department and graduated from Goddard College with a Bachelor of Individualized Studies.

WEBSITE: CAYENNEDOUGLASS.COM

THE MONOLOGUE:

Bush:

(Late 50s - Early 60s. Wise with a sense of humor. Her emotions are on the surface, a sensitive soul. She may struggle with mental illness. Please note the speech pattern of BUSH is written to reflect the number of teeth she has, not her race.)

I had a baby... but gave her up. It was the hardest thing I ever had to do. When she came outta me it was like a million little love needles stabbing me all over. I kept her fa three months. Ya know, dey say babies don't open der eyes right away but she come out, her eyes wide open. She was so interested. In everythin'. She was a good baby. A real good baby. It's as if she had a knowin'. It's as if she knew dat I was doing everythin' I could to try to... Old soul she was. I was tryin' ta keep her. Ta do right by her. But one day. It was da winter and she was hungry real like. Dey show me how to breas' feed but sometimes I can get no milk ta come out. Dey have programs where you can get formula for yo baby so I wen ta da clinic ta get it but day was jus closin'. I banged on th'door but no one come... so I wen out back, I know dey throw away some good things der. I foun me a can, neva been open, so I put dat in her bottle and feed it real nice, her eyes lookin' up at me. She wen ta sleep an I felt good... but den woke up like a half hour latter. Dis little itty bitty baby cryin', shakin'. Gettin' real hot den cold, real cold, at one point, lips turnin' blue… I took her ta the hospital, ta da emergency room. Dat der can was not good, was no good for her... dey fix her up so she fine again, but dey gave a talkin' ta me. Dey says, "I highly suggest you think about givin' her a future betta than your own." I thought a good future coulda bin wif me. I love her so much. But den I look at her: so fresh, wit everythin' before her. And I look at myself, an I realize, I was like dat garbage, I was dat spoiled milk. An' if she stay wif me I was gonna contaminate her. I wanted betta. Dat's wat every parent want for der child right? I wanted her to be somethin'... Maybe I could have. Maybe I would have if... but I couldn't see it den. An' if you can't see it, you can't do it. An' I had to make a choice dat wasn't selfish. Dey, at the hospital, dey set up an appointment wif a social worker lady, who explained da process. On da day I had to giv her up I got wit her in a little blue room ta say goodbye... She kep clingin' ta me but in a different way like... she always be knowin'... and when I handed her over we bof let out a cry... like at the same time. She kept cryin'. I put bof ma hands ova my mouth and walked out... but I didn't make it outta da building. I threw up in da lobby corner... Da social worker, she foun me. She stay wif me for a while. Put her hand on ma back. I didn' wanna be touched but I didn' say nuffin. "Take my card" she say, real formal like... like it... like it take the place of... They try an get you counselin' and I did it for a while... but I... I couldn't. I neva been the same after dat.

THE PLAY:

Woman Descending a Staircase

THE PLAYWRIGHT:

Phoebe Eaton

SYNOPSIS:

Sylvia Plath, thirty. Sylvia kills time as she awaits the return of her children and her estranged philandering fellow-poet husband Ted Hughes from a nearby zoo. Her philosophy of life, of death—of *art*—reveals itself as she toys with the idea of suicide.

ABOUT THE PLAYWRIGHT:

Phoebe Eaton is an award-winning playwright-screenwriter-investigative journalist.

A 2017 Helene Wurlitzer Foundation playwright fellow, she was a 2017-2018 Woodward/Newman Drama Award finalist with her play "Woman Descending a Staircase." A 2018 Imagine [Entertainment] Content Accelerator program finalist, her work has been developed at Naked Angels, Actors Studio Playwrights/Directors Unit, the Dramatists Guild, and the Kennedy Center. She has been a contributing feature writer to the *New York Times Magazine*, *New York* magazine, *Vanity Fair*, the *New York Observer*, *Harper's Bazaar,* and *The Daily Beast*, among others. 2017 New York Press Club Award. Scriptapalooza TV-writing prize. Member, Actors Studio Playwrights/Directors Unit. Dramatists Guild. B.A. University of Chicago.

WEBSITE: phoebeeaton.com

THE MONOLOGUE:

Sylvia:

My God, I've lost weight

I'm thinner now than before the babies

Childbirth is the biggest act of faith the body submits to

Bigger than giving yourself over to the custody of a husband

That's the No. 1 rule, having a child

You can't be who you *were*

I'm somebody's Mom now and Ted is

The Dad

He doesn't want the responsibility. He shirks. He blames

He finds others to take the risks *for* him

Coward

He didn't even leave me. It was I who took the

bull by the horns and showed him the door

I needed his mouth to

stop moving

Ted, the only upside to you lying all the time is I don't have to believe you when you say

You think you don't love me anymore

Life minus love equals a kind of death

Now, you can have a good death or a bad death

As young as I am

I'm only slightly in my 30s

I know I am fortunate to have a choice

My father had an ugly creeping death

The water basically rose and rose till it was over his nose but look

Mine will be stunning

Most people are walking around dead anyway

They just don't know it or want to acknowledge

They've let go the rope to themselves

Borne away in the dinghy of everybody else's wants and needs

Anyway, it's always been a direction I could go, this

Opting out

Doesn't scare me in the slightest, typing

The last period on the last page. A real writer, a true artist, knows when

the story's over

I was maybe 14? I was at the drugstore paging though *Life* magazine when

I saw something

So remarkable so

Staggering

I paid the 15 cents I was meant to spend on copy books and took the magazine home and hid it under the bed in the bedroom I was made to share with my mother

I would take it out when she wasn't around and just

Marvel at it

Like a spotty hormonal male who's got his greasy mitts on a Playboy left behind in a

garage somewhere

She was young, not so much older than me. A career girl in a little soignée suit and hosiery

Just recently engaged

She'd leapt from the 86th floor observation deck of the Empire State Building and

crash-bam-*slammed*

into the roof of a

shiny black Cadillac

Which now gathered her into its folds. It looked like somebody popped open a ring box

And there she was

An expression of pure bliss gleaming on her face

A nun's ecstasy, her first and final orgasm

A perfect ending, handed to the world in

white gloves. In her dash to the finish, no time to peel them off

Her hand at her throat, clutching at her

Collar of stringed pearls

Marriage wasn't for her, clearly

I mean, who's it for, really?

I had thought me

Well, apparently I was wrong

That man downstairs

He thinks I'm a snob

He does!

He is not the only one but anyway

Credit where it's due

This little bookkeeper from little suburban I think Tuckahoe?

In *Life* magazine!

Brava!

Not everyone can make art

THE PLAY:

Who You Calling A Bitch?!?

THE PLAYWRIGHT:

Sacha Elie

SYNOPSIS:

The famed Mammy character from Gone with the Wind. This is Mammy's response to the term "Bitch" and her role in African American cinematic history.

ABOUT THE PLAYWRIGHT:

Sacha Elie is a classically trained Haitian American actress, director, writer, and producer with an M.F.A. in Acting from UCLA's School of Theater Film and Television. Sacha made her OFF Broadway Debut in 2017 with one of her two solo pieces, 'Biscuits', of which she also directed. She is the proud recipient of the 2017 Hollywood Fringe Scholarship Award, where she received a nomination for The Rogue Machine's "Premiere" award for her second solo piece, also written, directed, produced by Sacha in "Who You Calling A Bitch?!?"! Which will receive its next reboot at the Whitefire Theater Solo Festival in Jan 2019. Some past performances include has performed in, A Midsummer Night's Dream (Williamstown Theater Festival), A Winter's Tale, (New Jersey Shakes Festival), Red Noses, (The Actors Gang), Fabulation or the Re-Education of Undine (West Coast Ensemble). Sacha has also toured both of her solo pieces in New York & L.A.

CONTACT: info@sachaelie.com

WEBSITE: sachaelie.com

THE MONOLOGUE:

Mammy:

"Oh My Lord, Lord, Lord" "Mmmmm Hmm".

Now I can't deny who I is any more then the sky can deny its blue.

Heck! Maybe, I was just written that way, heck maybe we all was just written the way we is, Child.

They say cause I'm big and Black that I must be ugly.

Some of them even say I hold no truth to what a real Negro woman is, some say because I came out of the mind of a white woman that I am a poor model to be admired.

Well, I wonder what that model is and should be, I reckon. Always setting such high bars for people like me, heck for woman like me. Why-, now Why can't I jus be me?

MMmmmm Hmm, Why, I do say things like I reckon. Yes mame. And am I always ready and willing to give a helping hand? Yes'um.

Now I don't understand all this fuss between Ms. Ray-Ray & Ms. Dominique. "If you are old enough to attend the party then you are old enough to act like ladies" is what I always say.

(Contemplates) Negro woman sure do fight each other these days. Fighting each other on those little o' silver screens. Jus tearing each other apart. Pulling on each others hair . . . cussing.

Its a shame to because every child is a child of God. Of Love. Now, I was born in hate, but I've never seen people needing so much love. What those girls need is GOD. OH! Hush! Now I know what you thinking, Most people don't believe in the good lord these days. Well now, shoot, not that many people believed in him in my time too. But what God showed us, was that God was love. Love was hope, and hope was the only thing that kept us alive. I don't think you can even imagine what it was like. Now shoot! Well, it looks like everyone has forgotten, anyhow, with the way things turning. History cycling around, intended to repeat itself, instead of trying something new.

Now I-I don't have the answers, but no matter what we do on that screen, it never seems to be enough something is always missing or hurting somebody. Well how about that somebody being me. No one ever wanting to take me on, while child, I is you. You's my kin, my own flesh and blood. You's my children . . . Now I want you to pray with me now, even if you don't believe in the good lord there is power in prayer you best believe. Cause on them days when all

43

you can see is what's in front of you, get down on them knees to give yourself peace, but most of all inspiration to find yourself again.

(sings)

"Oh My Lord, Lord, Lord" "Mmmmm Hmm".

(prays)

Dear Lord, Now I don't know much about women these days, but what I do know is that we women from where I came from held each other up. We protected each other from our masters . . . from the world.

We were each others sisters, daughters, mothers, lord you name it.

We gave one another love. Love for one self and Love for the other. But it was the women around me that showed me to choose love, so I gave it. Gave it to my masters, to my masters children. And so I'm giving it to you.

(sings)

"Oh My Lord, Lord, Lord" "Mmmmm Hmm".

Amen. Amen.

(she stands)

Now I'm proud to see my kin transform into the things you have become. Creating your own worlds, being the masters of your own future.

Its all prayed for, its all I sacrificed for. Now YOU don't get it twisted my poor children. I had to do things my soul cried against. But I did it for the future, so that one day, yes um, one day, a little girl, who looked like me, would one day look at me as beacon of hope and possibility. So that she can see how far she has come and how much further she can go. Dream. Big. My Children. Dream. Big. Dream bigger about yourself then you can ever imagine.

I did my best too, is all, and I guess they just doing theirs too. But somehow along the way we stopped loving each other. Being sisters for one another.

Now Ms. Dominique, Ms. Ray-Ray, oh now, it can't matter that much who was or is the first or best Black, "Bitch". What matters is what you give and— pass on, with dignity, pride and grace.

Now, I'm a Mammy an Aunt Jemima, unfit as black role model in black history, I, but you don't see that stopping me from being what I be. Just make sure you know why, my children, you calls yourself a Bitch—

THE PLAY:

Downsized

THE PLAYWRIGHT:

Anne Flanagan

SYNOPSIS:

Teri, a middle-aged Career Counselor for the Unemployment Office, has just been told
she's being laid off.

ABOUT THE PLAYWRIGHT:

Anne Flanagan's plays include Lineage, Artifice, First Chill, Skirts, Dark Holidays and Death, Sex & Elves. Her work has been produced throughout the US and internationally. Anne is the recipient of several writing awards and zero sports trophies. Publications include her comedy Artifice (Dramatic) as well as many short play and monologue anthologies.

Anne has taught public school in New York's South Bronx and LA's South Central. She's worked as a Private Investigator on the mean streets of Los Angeles (and the not so mean streets of Sherman Oaks). She's climbed Machu Picchu, used hot coffee as a weapon, had a gun pressed to her forehead, spied on thieving bartenders, built a house alongside Jimmy Carter, got lost in Watts holding a giant pineapple, and never mastered the metric system.

CONTACT: AngryTimmyPresents@yahoo.com

WEBSITE: anneflanagan.net

THE MONOLOGUE:

Teri:

I will not "have a nice day." No. Because I've just been laid off! That's what that call was about, I'm being laid off by the God Damned Unemployment Office! An unemployed career counselor - I don't know if that's irony or not but I sure as Hell know it sucks. I can't believe this - I've lost my job, my husband and - Huh? No. No, actually, I do NOT "still have my health." I have asthma. And high blood pressure and - Jesus! I'm three for three! Why is this happening to me?

All my life, I've been the 'good girl' and done things the 'right way' and what has it gotten me?! A cheating husband and a crap job - and I don't even have those anymore. What am I going to do?!

I'm forty four years old. What - I'm going to date? Are you joking?! Who's going to date me? I'm thirty pounds overweight, I'm unemployed, and I've started menopause. You realize I'll never have sex again, right? Even if I managed to hook someone willing, there's NO WAY I'm getting naked in front of them - and finding another job? HA!

Those pamphlets I just gave you about "not losing hope" and "There's a career waiting for you!"? Yeah, well, they're total bull. The job market is dead. DEEEEEEEEAD. I swear I am SO close to taking a blow torch to this hell hole - except I can't because I'll need to collect unemployment – OH NO - how humiliating is that going to be?! Oh God - I'm going to be one of them! I'm going to be one of those Mall Women. Standing by a kiosk, offering to buff your nails!

And now, another monologue from Anne Flanagan.

THE PLAY:

Lineage

SYNOPSIS:

Jessica, middle class and middle-aged, is a failed actor now trying to find her life's so called Second Act.

THE MONOLOGUE:

Jessica:

I was supposed to play Nancy on The Corporation, that sit com? But I didn't 'test' well with focus groups in the Midwest, which I would take as a huge compliment except that if they had liked me, my whole life would've changed. Or not. Anyway, the window of opportunity for women in Hollywood has a very, very narrow opening. I missed it. And now I'm a bit lost - I checked the Failed Actress Playbook but all the options: Yoga Teacher, Life Coach, Real Estate Agent – they suck.

There's also Marry a Rich Producer and/or become a Super Mom but I suck at sales and I married a middle class academic so... I've been tutoring and that feels... good, actually - and I've always liked photography but it's not my passion - though do I even have a passion? Or is that something you lose in middle age, along with your abs? Every self-help book -and I've read them all - they say "find your bliss" but maybe that's just another cliché like "Live each day as your last" - which is total bullshit; if you really lived each day like your last, you'd be fat and broke and probably on Death Row. I was passionate about acting but I wasn't, like, willing to be homeless to do it, but maybe I could have tried harder or hung in longer - then again, failure is as much my family's heritage as our eye color. It's in us, on a cellular level. We are a people steeped in defeat. Don't ask me why - I've downloaded every damn TED talk there is on failure but guess what? They're all given by highly successful people. There's never like a middle-aged swimmer who came thiiiis close to the Olympic team but now she coaches at the Y and lives in her brother's basement. No, instead there's Diana Nyad who's practically eighty and swam around the world. Or something like that. I want to hear from the past her prime swimmer, how does she get through the day with the chorus of "Loser! Loser!" blaring in her head? Everyone says "write a blog, start a podcast" but I've got nothing to write about and, really, the last thing this world needs is another fucking podcast.

THE PLAY:

Camouflage

THE PLAYWRIGHT:

Brenda Foley

SYNOPSIS:

Millie's quiet morning of fishing is disrupted by a stranger whose friendly demeanor hides a dark intent. Increasingly discomfited by his behavior, Millie confronts him in this culminating moment of the play.

ABOUT THE PLAYWRIGHT:

Brenda Foley's plays include Fallen Wings, Camouflage, Protocol, It's Not About the Crullers, Loyalty, The Code, Another New Year's Resolution, and Blood Pact. Her work has been produced and/or developed with, among others, the Boston Theater Marathon, Theatre Breaking Through Barriers, Sky Blue Theatre, NJ Theatre Project, The Wilbury Theatre Group, Camino Real Playhouse, Benchmark Theatre, and The Road Theatre Company. She was a 2017 Athena Theatre playwriting fellow and her full-length play, Fallen Wings, was selected for the Bechdel Group's 2017 New Play Development Reading Series. Protocol is published in The Best Ten-Minute Plays of 2018 (Smith and Kraus). Equity acting credits include the La Jolla Playhouse, Roundabout, Studio Arena, Alabama Shakespeare Festival, Indiana Rep, Pioneer Theatre, Philadelphia Drama Guild, NJ Theatre Project, GeVa Theatre, StageWest, Florida Stage, and Vienna's English Theatre. Brenda was named a winner of the British Theatre Challenge, is a recipient of the Carbonell Award for Best Actress, and is editor of the Routledge Series in Equity, Diversity, and Inclusion in Theatre and Performance. MFA: Cal Arts; PhD: Brown University.

CONTACT: bkfoleygard@gmail.com

WEBSITE: brendafoley.me

THE MONOLOGUE:

Millie:

The only "mistake" that's been made here is I've wasted ten minutes of my life I can never get back listening to you. You think I'm unaware that men like you come out in daylight just as often as they hide at night? Men who make themselves feel powerful by threatening women. Men who stop next to women waiting at crosswalks at ten in the morning on chilly fall days, who smile and say "I want to buy you breakfast," who take them by the elbow and shove them against an alley wall while all of Boston walks by, fifteen feet away from the cold brick. You accuse me of being inattentive but I paid attention that day. I paid attention to every detail so I would recognize that kind of man again when I encountered him. I paid attention to his breathing and his smell, to the button on his collar, to his arm across my chest and the scrape of his coat against my skin so the next time I would know him by the way he moves, the tone of his voice, his arrogance, and his evil. And that is how I'm able to recognize you. Women don't end up missing because we're "inattentive." We end our days discarded like broken toys in landfills and creek beds because men like you exist.

THE PLAY:

Secret Dreamers

THE PLAYWRIGHT:

Ed Friedman

SYNOPSIS:

Three sisters are spending the day at an art museum. Hannah, the youngest, is mesmerized by a particular work of art.

ABOUT THE PLAYWRIGHT:

Ed's short plays have been staged throughout the NY metropolitan area and around the country. They include Love at Worst Sight, Secret Dreamers, The Keys to Life? Smoke Gets in Your Eyes, It's Time, Mine/Ours, Two Ships, Out and About, and Let No Man Tear Asunder. His longer play The Prism has been produced by the Westchester Collaborative Theatre. His monologues are published in the anthologies of Mother/Daughter Monologues: MidLife Catharsis and Urgent Maturity published by the International Centre for Women Playwrights.

CONTACT: adlib501@hotmail.com

THE MONOLOGUE:

Hannah:

(Lights dim on all but Hannah. We hear the soft strains of "Clair de Lune")

The woman on the right, Jacqueline, has left her mansion in the south of France. She's told her husband she's off to visit her friend Cecile. While this is true, it doesn't matter to the husband as his attentions are consumed with his business interests and his latest affair with a young female flight attendant. Had he paid any attention while Jacqueline was getting ready, he would have seen that she wore nothing underneath her dress except stockings. She's on fire with excitement as she drives to the edge of the forest at the outskirts of town. Jacqueline has arranged to meet her lover outside the remains of an abandoned castle. She and Cecile have been lovers for six months. Their desire for each other is boundless, pushing past their inhibitions far further than either would have imagined. Cecile has told Jacqueline that tonight they would take their passion for each other even further. Jacqueline can't even imagine this. Her anticipation has her heart racing. Her desire causes her to drive much faster than she would ordinarily. When she gets to the abandoned castle she literally leaps from the car and walks swiftly to the appointed place. Jacqueline finds her lover, bathed in moonlight, naked except for a bed of leaves. She is flush with excitement as Cecile says, "Have you done as I asked?" "Yes", Jacqueline replies. Cecile says, "Take your dress off now". Jacqueline hesitates. "Here?" "Yes, here and now" Cecile says as she brushes the leaves off her body revealing herself completely. Jacqueline, mesmerized, removes her own dress. "Come to me", Cecile whispers. Jacqueline moves to her lover as they embrace, both bathed in moonlight. Their passion breathing life into the long abandoned structure that surrounds them. *(Music out. Lights as before. Hannah is out of her reverie, matter of factly)* Well, that's just what I see. Ready for lunch? *(Hannah walks out. Lee and Holly look at each other, mouths open.)*

THE PLAY:

Amparo

THE PLAYWRIGHT:

Vanessa Garcia

SYNOPSIS:

Edna, a woman trying to escape Cuba after the Revolution. She's trying to get out and hiding her most prized possession. The entire thing takes place in a bathroom stall before a strip search.

ABOUT THE PLAYWRIGHT:

Vanessa Garcia is a multidisciplinary artist working as a novelist, playwright, and journalist. Her debut novel, White Light, was published in 2015, to critical acclaim. It was named one of NPR'S Best Books of 2015 and won an International Latino Book Award. She holds a PhD from the University of California Irvine in English (with a focus in Creative Nonfiction), an MFA from the University of Miami (in fiction), and a BA from Barnard College, Columbia University (English and Art History).

Her plays have been produced in Edinburgh, Miami, Los Angeles, New York, and other cities around the world. These include The Cuban Spring (a full-length Carbonell Award nominee for Best New Play, 2015), The Crocodile's Bite (a short included in numerous anthologies such as Smith & Kraus' Best Ten Minute Plays of 2016; the City Theatre Anthology 2015; and the Writer's Digest Annual Award Anthology, 2015), and Freek!, a short play for Young Adults (anthologized in The Applause Acting Series' 5 Minute Plays For Teens). As a journalist, feature writer, and essayist, her pieces have appeared in The LA Times, The Miami Herald, The Guardian, The Washington Post, Narrative.ly, The Southern Humanities Review, The Huffington Post, and numerous other publications. Most recently she was a Sesame Street Writer's Room Fellow, is currently a WP Theatre Lab fellow, and is a Professor of Writing at SCAD (Savannah College of Art and Design).

WEBSITE: vanessagarcia.org

THE MONOLOGUE:

Edna:

[In a bathroom stall, Edna stares, for a moment, at the locket necklace she's holding]

See. Inside here, there. It's empty now, but a pearl goes there. My best friend Margarita has it. She's a dancer and an actress, she's going somewhere else. She's trying to get on a plane to the United States. "straight to the United States," she says, "forget the rest, New York City, that's it." She has big dreams. I have family in Spain, so I have to go there, but oh how I wish we were going together. On this trip, on this, this...new adventure.

Me and Margarita, we've been friends forever. Since we were kids. You know the kind. The kind you scrape your knees with, cheat on exams with, bitch about your mother with, talk about the boys with, call right after you lose your virginity.

[She takes out a brand new Kotex, a pad, from her bag, unwraps it, flattens it out near the sink]

Oh God, I don't even want to remember that. We actually lost our virginity to the same person. We planned it. Manuel was his name. He was our friend and we thought: Why not, right? He's got what we don't have, that's all we need, let's get this over with. [Laughs]

Poor Manuel, had no idea, thought he was scoring big, two girls, one week apart. Margarita went on a Friday, I let her go first, and then the next Friday it was my turn. I was scared shitless.

[As she cuts through the Kotex and buries the necklace inside the clean cushion of the cotton, stuffs it way back in the pad, so it doesn't get in the way]

They say they strip you, you know, before you get on the plane. They take you away to a little corner and they strip you, make you take your clothes off, except your underwear. They won't look here.

[She has a long dress on, so as she puts the pad on her panty, we don't have to see anything indecent, but we definitely feel we are witnessing a very personal moment]

Anyway... Margarita has the pearl that used to go inside the necklace. Said that way we'd have a piece of each other forever.

[Pulls the panty up, long skirt covers the action...like when you are changing and trying to hide...like you do in a locker room]

Because the world is big, you know, and you don't know, you never know, if we'll ever see each other again.

THE PLAY:

Tamar (The Two-Gated City)

THE PLAYWRIGHT:

Emma Goldman-Sherman

SYNOPSIS:

Tamar (The Two-Gated City) is a play with music that incorpo-rates 2 rape culture stories from the Bible (Tamar's story in Samuel II and the story of the Concubine in Judges 19) in a story about a young woman who is trying to find out the truth about her aunt for whom she was named. In this monologue, Aunt Tamar, based on the original Tamar from Samuel II, testifies.

ABOUT THE PLAYWRIGHT:

Emma Goldman-Sherman's plays include wombshot, Perfect Women (Jane Chambers Award), MAN & WIFE, and ZEN & the Art of Mourning a Mother. Other work produced in the UK, Australia, Croatia, Canada, NYC and regionally across the US. She earned her MFA from the University of Iowa where she won the Richard Maibaum Award for plays addressing social justice. She is the Resi-dent Dramaturg at the 29th Street Playwrights Collective where she runs the WriteNow Workshop. Member: Dramatists Guild.

CONTACT: emmagoldmansherman@gmail.com, 646-260-8102

WEBSITE: 29thstreetplaywrightscollective.org

newplayexchange.org/users/1088/emma-goldman-sherman

THE MONOLOGUE:

Aunt Tamar:

I offered him the food I made

but instead he grabbed my wrist

he said, Come lie with me, my sister,

56

and no brother was he then

and gripped me hard - my bread fell

and yet I remained calm and spoke to him

No, my brother, I said

thinking to remind him of himself

the fact of our birth

Do not violate me I said for it is not done thus

I spoke reasonably without invoking God or my feelings

we all know how men disdain our feelings

Do not do this foolish thing, I said

as if I might appeal to his manliness

the idea that he might want to appear to be reasonable

and still he held me hard so I spoke again,

I, where would I carry my shame?

No pockets in my virgin dress

No way to become anything else

You, I told him, you would be like a fool,

and still no change, so I mentioned our father, the king,

Now speak to the king, for he will not keep me from you.

But he did not want to hear my voice

He wanted only to feast his eyes on me

He wanted only to touch me

so even though I spoke wisely, he refused to hear me.

And now, another monologue from Emma Goldman-Sherman.

The Play:

Fukt

Synopsis:

Fukt is a memoir-play about traumatic memory where Emma is played by 3 actors (who also play many other characters) in a kind of one-woman show where Barbara, at this point in the play, tells the audience how she changed her name to Emma, and Emma, played by another actor, is onstage with Barbara, having just integrated the truth about all the different parts of herself - including the part called "Barbara" - and the trauma they have lived through. Emma lets Barbara tell this final part of the story, and then Barbara is supposed to let Emma move on.

The Monologue:

Barbara:

(to audience)

A man on a date, as you all probably know, does not get to re-name a person and it's done. I was not permanently re-christened in that bar. A year later, when we were getting married, we went to the Diamond District on 47th Street to get our rings engraved. In a room full of Hasidic men, under huge black hats, with payess - ringlets - hanging from their temples, each behind a counter like in a department store only it's not chandeliered, it's fluorescent and shabby. We found an engraver who asked us to write down what we wanted engraved, and we handed them in. And the engraver read them both and nodded and started to engrave my ring with what my husband had written: Love Forever Scott. And while this was happening, I was standing there thinking, I'm having a baby with this man - I'm already pregnant and puking for this man - I love this man. I am going to make this work forever with this man. I want to be his. And he calls me Emma. And I wrote Barbara on the piece of paper for the man to engrave. So I turned to the man, and said, Excuse me, can I change what I wrote? And the man shrugged. He

58

doesn't want to talk to me. I'm a woman. These men only like to deal with other men. They make that very clear. Can I change it? So he put the paper back on the counter. And I hunched over it so my husband wouldn't see the surprise. And I crossed out Barbara and wrote down Emma. And I handed it back to the man. And he read it. And all I could do was imagine his thoughts —

(as Hasidic Engraver)

Who does she think she is? She doesn't even know her real name? She doesn't know what he calls her? What does he call her? Crazy? Who writes the wrong name? In all the years I'm working here, who has ever put the wrong name? Why would she do that? Doesn't she know who she is? What is the matter with her? And now she's laughing so hard, I think she'll piss herself. Meshuguh!

(as herself, laughing, and eventually directly to Emma)

And I laughed until the tears squeezed out of my eyes and rolled down my cheeks, and I had to squat down on the ugly carpet to keep from pissing myself. And Scott thought I'd lost my mind, but I was so happy, I felt such joy, because I knew I could be you - in that moment, I became you!

THE PLAY:

Seal Song

THE PLAYWRIGHT:

Jennifer Fell Hayes

SYNOPSIS:

Nora has been living by the sea with her elderly mother, who has just died. She is drying off after her morning swim, remembering a recent unusual encounter she has had with a seal.

ABOUT THE PLAYWRIGHT:

Jennifer Fell Hayes, a playwright with New York's Workshop Theater Company, has written plays including Rosemary and Time (Paradise Factory Theatre, 2018) and A Weekend in Filey (Workshop Theater Company, 2011 and Hen and Chickens, London, 2014). Seal Song was first performed at the Samuel French Short Play Festival (where it was a semi-finalist) and then at the Midtown International Theatre Festival on a double bill called Seal Songs. She has written many plays for youth and museums, co-authored an award-winning book, Pioneer Journeys, about drama in museum education, and is published by Samuel French and the Dramatic Publishing Company. A member of the Dramatists Guild, Jennifer is English and divides her time between Yorkshire and New York City.

CONTACT: Fellhayes@aol.com

WEBSITE: fellhayes.wixsite.com/home

THE MONOLOGUE:

Nora:

(to audience): No seal today. I go to the library and take out a book on seals, and I find out they can go forty miles without taking a breath. Imagine! And they can dive to a depth of over two thousand feet. What remarkable creatures they are. The woman at the library is very kind.

She says she'll find me some more books on seals. Of course she's known me a long time, now. I used to get a lot of books for Mother. She liked Regency romances - I believe they call them bodice rippers. I had to laugh. She was such a mild, little old lady, with a nimbus of white hair. And then she'd read those books about highwaymen and courtesans, bloody duels and heaving bodices, looking as meek as you please sitting in her favorite pink armchair. Sometimes I didn't know where to look when I returned them. I used to wait until the women were busy with other customers, and then slide them back into the returns pile. I did! Well, I didn't want them to think I read such things.

I look at her armchair now, when I'm reading. Sometimes I pretend she's still in it. If I half shut my eyes, and squint a bit, I can almost see her fragile shape, glasses perched on her nose. She had beautiful eyes, blue as cornflowers, and even just before she - *(she clears her throat momentarily)* they didn't fade much. Some old people's eyes do, don't they? They fade into a sort of dirty water color. Mother's never did.

(She looks out to sea)

Beautiful light this morning, isn't it? There's a sort of sheen on the sea's face. I love the morning light, it's so much more subtle than later in the day. I wonder where the seal is now?

And now, another monologue from Jennifer Fell Hayes.

THE PLAY:

Seal Song

SYNOPSIS:

Nora has been living by the sea with her elderly mother, who has just died. She has found a beautiful nightgown amongst her mother's things.

THE MONOLOGUE:

Nora:

(to audience) I'm clearing away a last bag of Mother's things, and I come across her best nightdress.

(Holds it out)

I gave it to her for Christmas one year - it's gorgeous. Pink satiny, fabric, beautiful soft lace ribbons - the works. She loved it. She oohed and aahed over it all day, and I'd find her stroking it, and holding it up against her in front of the mirror. It was a big hit. She said it was too good to wear for every day, and she kept right on wearing the old faded cotton nighties she always wore. She put the satin nightgown, beautifully folded, into a clear, sealed plastic bag, and put that into a little night case with some pretty slippers she'd never worn. She said it was in case she had to go in hospital. I found the nightie still there yesterday.

(A beat. She strokes the nightie, holds it to her cheek).

I was going to send it to the undertakers, for her to wear in the coffin she went in to the crematorium. She'd told me firmly she wanted to be cremated, not take up more space in an overcrowded churchyard. But when I thought about it, I realized she would have hated the thought of that beautiful nightgown going up in flames. I could hear her voice in my head, what a shocking waste, Nora! So I put it back in the bag, and that's where I found it yesterday.

(A beat. She holds the nightie tenderly in her arms a moment).

She never even wore it once!

THE PLAY:

Nightie Night

THE PLAYWRIGHT:

Elayne Heilveil

SYNOPSIS:

Jule, twenties, raised in the Bayou, has a sudden memory of her beloved childhood puppet, Nightie Night, which she lost years ago in the swamp. She has rushed back to find it, but when she's there she recalls the memories of her loss and has to confront the dreaded 'Monster in the Mud' to reveal the mystery of her past.

ABOUT THE PLAYWRIGHT:

Elayne Heilveil is an actress, journalist, director and award-winning playwright. As an actress she's starred in numerous theatre, film and television productions. As a playwright her many competition-winning short plays have been produced throughout the country. She is published by Dramatic Publishing Company, Smith and Kraus and Applause Cinema & Theatre Books. Publications in some recent anthologies include; "Best Contemporary Monologues (Age 7-15; 2015); "More 10-Minute Plays for Teens (2015); "Best Ten-Minute Plays" (2016; Smith & Kraus); "Best Ten-Minute Plays" (2016); "Best Ten-Minute Plays" (2017); "Best Women's Stage Monologues" (2017); "Best Ten-Minute Plays" (2018). Her most recent short play was produced in Australia and recorded for radio. She is a graduate of New York's High School for The Performing Arts and Carnegie Mellon University.

CONTACT: Elayne Heilveil, 310 471-0778, elaynerh@aol.com

THE MONOLOGUE:

Jule:

I was just a baby in a crib. There was a draft out the window one night. The curtains waved.

And the sound of leaves were crushin' under foot. And the cat, my Nightie Night, who purred me to sleep, whose paw tapped gently on the cradle as it rocked me back and forth until I'd drift safely into slumber under some sea of stars and I would float away in a cotton candy cloud of dreams—- disappeared.

(To the unseen 'Monster'.)

Did you take Nightie Night from me? Were his tiny bones buried in the mud for the flies to eat? Did he see you when he leapt out the window to chase your footsteps in the dark? Did the leaves crush under your feet? The wind howl with your breath or the rain weep with tears like… soiled sweat?

(She wipes her forehead as if feeling the humidity and a memory she can't place.)

Momma said she could never sleep for my cries after that. The cries from baby me that Nightie Night would soothe. "Hush," Momma'd say when I couldn't sleep. "You want the Thing to take you too? The Thing that takes the souls who are scared and sucks their life and leaves 'em in the dark?"After that, I didn't cry, or scream or barely talk at all—- accept to the socks. "Where did all the socks go?" Momma would say. "Did they get swallowed and eaten up by the broken down machine?"

(Smiles; proudly remembering.)

I made him come alive again. I did. My Nightie Night. Out of sox. And threads for whiskers, and buttons, black, for eyes. And I'd tell him things no one else could know. I'd whisper things, and he'd talk back, in secret puppet talk to me.

(Pause. Remembering.)

I had him all those years, all those years of secrets, that got buried somewhere in the slime, with the flies, in the water, drowned by the monster in the mud? And now that I am old, or old enough to know, I need to find him. To tell him — something nice happened tonight. Something good.

(Proud, innocent.)

I got kissed. I did. A young man said I was pretty. And smart. And under a sweet yellow moon, we danced. Around and around…

(She looks up and whirls, as if to bring the moment back.)

… and I looked up at a string of sparkling lights, like stars winkin' a Hallelujah chorus, somethin' sweet and kind and oh suddenly I felt nice and clean and good… Yes, for a moment, I did. Feel. Something. Good. And I closed my eyes, and I drifted into a dream of wonder and suddenly I was back with my Nightie Night, floatin' on that cotton candy cloud with a crown of stars above my head, like I had on my crib? Only tonight, I was floatin' for real. I was alive.

(Beat; the flashes of memory coming back.)

For a moment, I was…Then words, pictures, like pieces in an unfinished puzzle exploded in my head.

(Beat; calling out to 'Monster'.)

Did you take Nightie Night from me!?

THE PLAY:

Great Roles for Old Actresses

THE PLAYWRIGHT:

Andrew R. Heinze

SYNOPSIS:

June (openly lesbian) addresses the other women. Previously the others knew that June has a tormenting relationship with her daughter, but she had refused to reveal anything about that.

ABOUT THE PLAYWRIGHT:

Formerly a professor of American History and nonfiction author, Andrew has been a playwright for ten years. His plays have been produced in NYC, LA, Seattle, Austin, Miami, Denver, Albuquerque and regionally. Andrew's full-length plays include DELETING DAD (Winner, Texas NonProfit Theatres' 2016 New Play competition); THE INVENTION OF THE LIVING ROOM (Winner, Texas Non-Profit Theatres' 2014 New Play competition; Finalist–First Runner-Up, 2012 Blue Ink Playwriting Award); MOSES, THE AUTHOR (2014 NYC Fringe Festival & Fringe Encore Selection); PLEASE LOCK ME AWAY (Finalist, 2012 Kitchen Dog Theater New Works Competition). His one-act plays include: THE FQ (published in Smith & Kraus's The Best Ten-Minute Plays, 2011) and THE BAR MITZVAH OF JESUS GOLDFARB (Winner, Judges Choice & Audience Choice, Best Play, 17th Annual New York City Fifteen-Minute Play Festival; Finalist, 2018 National Award for Short Playwriting). Member, Dramatists Guild of America.

WEBSITE: andrewheinze.com

THE MONOLOGUE:

June:

What is it with bleeding and women? Men shoot, they knife, they punch, each other, or us – they make other people bleed. But women, we make ourselves bleed. What is that? A cry for help?

Help! My period! My body is expelling part of me. Help! My arms! I'm cutting them because I can't feel at all. Or because I feel too much. Help! My pillow! It's turning red because I'm a drug addict and I can't tell my mother.

For months I thought she just had an allergy, all the sniffling. And blood, well, you do the laundry and you don't necessarily think anything of it when you see some blood on a pillow, and I didn't, until the day I did.

And when I said, "Why don't you stop?" she cries out, her little voice – it seemed suddenly so little – choking and trembling from tears, her chest – the same little chest that I bathed in the bassinet the day before yesterday – now heaving as she cries out to me, to me, and I never heard a cry for help like this, so desperate, so desperate: "I WANT to stop but I CAN'T!" She wants to but she can't. She can't. She tries rehab and she stops, I can do this on my own, and she tries and she stops. She can't get through to the other side. She can't. And me. What do I do now? What? I'm not helping her. I drop everything if she needs me, I pick up every phone call in case it's the last, I pay bills she can't pay, and this is a capable person, a gifted person. I'm not helping her. I make her worse.

> *(Kim: She's used to the attention, she wants it. Maybe there's a way to help her without her getting— without you paying too much attention?)*

> *(enraged)*

A mother can't pay too much attention! Bad things don't happen from too much attention! Bad things happen from looking the other way! Bad things happen when mothers pretend not to notice what the family doctor is doing when he's reaching under a little dress to make sure "everything is all right!" Bad things happen when a little girl tries in her pathetic, ashamed little way to make it stop, when I begged not to go to Dr. Wells anymore because Dr. Wells was scary and I was told not to be so dramatic, you're so dramatic, this family has always gone to Dr. Wells, it's all in your head, it's all in your mind!

> *(pause)*

I always wanted to be a mother. I didn't want a man, a husband, I didn't want that. Not because of Dr. Wells, if that's what you're thinking, not because of him. I just love women. I always loved women. But I wanted to be a mother. And when I did what I had to do to become a mother, I knew two things. I knew I wanted a little girl and I knew I would always pay attention. I was blessed with a little girl, and I always paid attention. And now I'm helping her kill herself.

THE PLAY:

Old Men And Fig Newtons

THE PLAYWRIGHT:

Linda LaRocque

SYNOPSIS:

Years, memories and Luther's tragic, untimely death, have taken a heavy toll on aging Cappy. For reasons known only to her, she recounts openly and without regret, the double life she shared between a cruel, lonely marriage and a long-term love affair.

ABOUT THE PLAYWRIGHT:

An award-winning playwright, Linda's scripts are available through Playscripts, Art Age Publishing, and Contemporary Drama Service. She is also a frequent contributor to the Chicken Soup for the Soul series.

CONTACT: Linda.l.larocque@gmail.com

269-637-3416
616-405-3001

THE MONOLOGUE:

Cappy:

You're probably wonderin' who'd ever find me, old Cappy Johnson attractive, right? Well, I didn't always look like this. Karl never said I was pretty. (She removes her cap and touches her hair gently) Fact is, he never said much of anything nice to me. So, when Luther Ramsey, came along, with that coal black hair and Irish charm, I fell — all the way.

Karl never knew. He wouldn't have cared anyway. All he ever had time for was the bottle. But Luther had time for me, even crewin' on the ore freighter, didn't keep us apart for long. I should've left Karl, but back then, you didn't divorce. You stayed for the kids. Couldn't put them through more shame. Bad enough their dad was the town drunk. Oh, I thought about leavin', all right. Even planned it once, but chickened out at the last minute.

Day of Karl's funeral, after everybody went home, kids were still there, and we all ended up sittin' around the dinin' room table, talkin'. Same table we'd had a thousand meals at. And you know what? The kids said they wondered why I stayed with their Dad all them years. Can you imagine that? All along, I thought they wanted me to stay, and all along, they wanted me to leave.

I never told them about Luther. No reason to. It was between me and him. But I sure got some beautiful memories.

I knew it wasn't right, us not being married and all.

But he made me feel like a woman and I'd do it all over again.

We had breakfast together the mornin' he left for Duluth. I was waitin' table at the truck stop, and when I got off, Luther was standin' by the door. Wanted to tell me good bye before he got on the bus, like he always did.

Bus was late, cause it was snowin' and pilin' up fast, so Luther hurried and got on. The bus pulled away and I just stood there. Land, how I cried when he left. I know you won't believe it and I've never told another soul either, but I knew somethin' bad was gonna happen. I ran back into the diner and tried wipin' the steam off the window so I could get one last glimpse of him as the bus pulled away. *(Pause)* Somethin' told me. *(Pause)* I just felt it in my gut. *(Pause)* A week later, one of the cooks heard it over the radio. She came a screamin' out from the kitchen and told us, *(Pause)* the Edmund Fitzgerald, *(Pause)* the freighter Luther was on .... sank off Whitefish Bay.... and all twenty-nine crewmen and captain ....were lost at sea.

THE PLAY:

A Birthday Party

THE PLAYWRIGHT:

Mark Harvey Levine

SYNOPSIS:

Jen would like you to know she's not homeless. She's a Birthday Party.

ABOUT THE PLAYWRIGHT:

Mark Harvey Levine has had over 1600 productions of his plays everywhere from Bangalore to Bucharest and from Lima to London. His work has been produced at such theaters as the Actors Theatre of Louisville and City Theatre of Miami. His plays have won over 35 awards and been produced in ten languages. He has had 14 plays published in volumes of "The Best Ten Minute Plays" over the years and 3 other monologues also published in Smith & Kraus Anthologies.

Full evenings of his plays, such as "Cabfare For The Common Man", "Didn't See That Coming" and "A Very Special Holiday Special" have been shown in New York, Amsterdam, Edinburgh Fringe Festival, Sao Paulo, Sydney, Seoul, Mexico City, and across the US. A Spanish-language movie version of his play "The Kiss" ("El Beso") premiered at Cannes, showed at the Tribeca film festival, and subsequently aired on HBO and DTV (Japan).

CONTACT: markle96@hotmail.com

WEBSITE: markharveylevine.com

THE MONOLOGUE:

Jen:

(On the street. JEN is waiting with balloons which can say "Happy Birthday" on them and lots of grocery bags. She notices people staring at her.)

Hi... Oh... I'm just waiting for someone. I'm not... I mean, I'm not a homeless person or anything. Not that there's anything wrong with being homeless. Well, except that you don't have a home. I just mean, I don't hate the homeless or anything. I'm not a...*(searches for the right word, then pathetically)* homelessist. It's just that people have been mistaking me for one. Seriously. A lady came by and gave me a dollar. It's all the bags, I think. Anyway. I'm just waiting for someone. —I gave her the dollar back!

He's probably not even going to show. I get that a lot. Do you? You make a date with a guy, you're going to meet him, and they never show up. I should probably just let these balloons free, and go home.

Okay, really — have you ever seen a homeless person with balloons? I have balloons. I am holding Happy Birthday balloons in my hand. And a lot of groceries. I'm a birthday party! See?

Yes, right here in all these bags, is everything you need for a great birthday party. It's for this guy, Stephen. It's our first date. And his birthday was actually a week ago. But I thought it would be fun, right? To surprise him. To throw him a little birthday party right there at the restaurant. I have everything. Balloons. Party hats. Those noise-maker blower thingies. I even got a cake, that says "Happy Birthday Stephen" on it.

Which was like the hardest part, because I didn't actually know if he was a Steven with a "V" or a Stephen with a "PH"? So I went to his apartment building really late one night, to see if his name was written on his mailbox or something? And it was! It said "S. Rosen". Great.

So I actually looked in the dumpster behind the place to see if I could find a magazine or an envelope or something with his name on it. I had to dig through a lot of trash! It was disgusting. But I did find a bunch of his mail and it's Stephen with a "PH". Plus he's a little behind on his Visa payments.

I'm not a stalker! I'm just a careful speller. And I mean wouldn't it suck to get a birthday cake with your name spelled wrong on it?

I just hope he didn't see me rooting around in his dumpster. That would've been weird. For him, too, I guess. Actually I'm really paranoid he's seen me here, with the balloons. My deepest fear is that he was circling the block, looking for a parking spot, and saw me standing here with all the groceries and the balloons and decided I was a crazy person and took off. Just drove away as fast as his car could take him.

I don't know what his car looks like. I peeked in all the cars at his building after I went through the garbage but I couldn't figure out which one was his. So I don't have that information.

But he's already a half an hour late. It is hard to find parking sometimes. But still. I should just forget the whole thing. Let the balloons go. Give up. Maybe I try too hard. But isn't that what you would like in a relationship? Someone who tries? Hard? I know I would.

It's okay, I'm sure he'll be here any second. Don't worry about me. Go and do whatever it is you're doing. Anyway, I just wanted you to know... I'm not a homeless person. I'm a birthday party! I'm a birthday party...

(She gives them a brave smile. She waits.)

THE PLAY:

Temptress Standing by an Open Window

THE PLAYWRIGHT:

Paul Lewis

SYNOPSIS:

A down-on-his luck builder meets an alluring yet mysterious mindreader in a bar. Unable to place her accent, he asks her what country she is from.

ABOUT THE PLAYWRIGHT:

Paul Lewis is a Seattle-based playwright and composer whose projects include a musical adaptation of The Runaway Bunny (Boston Children's Theatre); The Crossing, A Musical (Theater Schmeater and Jewel Box Theatre), winner of a Seattle Times Footlight Award for promising new work; a musical adaptation of Caps for Sale (Boston Children's Theatre); the full-length play Oblivion (Driftwood); and The Hours of Life, A Musical (Theatre22). His play The Names has had recent developmental readings at FUSION, Equity Library Theatre Chicago, and Atlantic Stage. Paul's one-act plays have been staged at theatres across the U.S., winning Best of Festival awards at a number of these. Member of the Dramatists Guild of America.

CONTACT: writing.musicals@gmail.com, 206 953 4120

WEBSITE: paullewis.work

THE MONOLOGUE:

Princess Doraldina:

What country? you ask. No single country, but many countries. I am the Princess of the midway, the carnival, the penny arcade, brought to life amongst the scent of rosewood and mahogany and gun oil, at the Roover Brothers Novelty Company of Philadelphia. It was the Roover Brothers who manufactured and named me and sent me out into the world — Princess Doraldina the Fortune Teller. For more than a century I traveled the world in my glass and mahogany home, and watched as an endless parade of solitary souls — men mostly, sailors, hustlers, students and hoboes — stood before my fortune-telling machine to try to untangle the riddle of their lives. Their fortunes I could not predict. That task belonged to the gears of the machine. But I soon found that I could hear their thoughts through the glass just as clearly as I can hear your voice. As each stood waiting for his appointed fate to unwind from the spool of the machine, they could see the pity in my eyes, even through the smudged and dusty glass. They could see that I was listening, and they grew still. And in that moment they confessed their every secret, unburdened the inchoate longings and desires of a lifetime. The town drunk remembered his long-abandoned dreams of greatness. The righteous citizens, their long-hidden crimes. There is barely enough space in all the world to contain all these stories and all these secrets. I know you think I am crazy. Of course I am crazy. Crazy with pathos. Mad with tenderness. Who would not go crazy after listening to all of the secret thoughts of a great and terrible century on earth?

True Acting Institute

The Play:

Exceeding The Purchasable Calories

The Playwright:

Rhea MacCallum

Synopsis:

In a quest for comfort food one woman discovers the importance of reading the fine print. At her wit's end, she makes a final plea to acquire her desired purchase.

About The Playwright:

Rhea MacCallum is an award-winning playwright, screenwriter and script consultant, whose plays have been produced across the United States and six continents. Her work has been published by Smith & Kraus, Heuer Publishing, Original Works, Pioneer Drama and themonologueshop.com. She is a member of the Dramatists Guild, ICWP, ALAP, Playground-LA's Writer's Pool and Skylight Theatre's PlayLAb. BA: USC; MFA in Playwriting: Actors Studio Drama School/New School for Drama, New School University in New York City.

CONTACT: rheamac@yahoo.com

WEBSITE: rheamaccallum.com

The Monologue:

Woman:

You've got to be kidding me. What if I just had a crap filled day? What about that? Maybe I started my day by stepping on cat puke and followed that up by stubbing my big toe on my coffee table causing the nail to nearly come completely off. Then I missed my train to work, showed up late and, of course, it turned out to be a performance review day so my boss, my bosses boss and my bosses bosses boss all watched me hobble my way into the office and just when I thought I couldn't be any more embarrassing I look down and realize that the buttons on my blouse aren't matching up and there's this huge gap where anyone with eyes can see my bra and naturally I'm wearing the backup, dingy, should have thrown it out three years ago bra. You ever try to re-button your blouse while trying to avoid being caught doing it? Impossible. Then during my performance review I realize no one on the panel of my supervisors will look me in the eye and I think maybe it's just me, maybe I'm being paranoid, I mean, I'm decent looking. Why will no one look me in the eye, I wonder, and when I leave the room I hear them erupt into laughter so I go to the bathroom to go cry in the third stall and that's when I see this dry crusted huge snot wad just hanging at the edge of my nostril, just dangling there as if suspended in air. Then I spend the whole day paranoid that every snicker, every sideways glance is about what a train wreck of a person I've become and I just want it all to stop. So yeah, maybe chips and wine and ice cream and donuts is not the greatest thing I could do for myself right now, but it's what I need to help me forget this disastrous day. Maybe it's all crap that I would be better off without, but right now it's all I have to stop me from wanting to die. These are the things that make my life tolerable.

THE PLAY:

Fata Morgana

THE PLAYWRIGHT:

Jeni Mahoney

SYNOPSIS:

When Tori's teenage niece, Morgan, shows up pregnant and asks her Aunt Tori and Uncle Jack to adopt her unborn baby, it seems like the answer to their long held dreams. In this monologue, Tori needs to enlist the help of her friend Shelley (a nurse) who has only just arrived at Tori's house to find Morgan dead in the garage and Tori terrified of losing a baby she has already risked everything to save.

ABOUT THE PLAYWRIGHT:

Jeni Mahoney is a playwright, director, dramaturg and play development geek. She has written more than a dozen plays including: Fata Morgana, The Feast of the Flying Cow… and Other Stories of War, Mercy Falls, Kandahar, Come Rain or Come Shine, Scatter and Light which have been seen at venues around the country including: The National Playwrights Conference, L.A. Theater Center, Key City Public Theater, Boston Theater Marathon, Rattlestick Theater, the Lark and Boise Contemporary Theater, where Fata Morgana was honored with an NEA Artworks Grant. Jeni is the Founding Artistic Director of Seven Devils Playwrights Conference and Producing Artistic Director id Theater. Directing credits include the National Winter Playwrights Retreat, Key City Public Theater and the Durango PlayFest. An inductee in the Indie Theater Hall of Fame, Jeni also serves on the Board of Trustees for the National Theatre Conference and is a member of the Dramatists Guild.

CONTACT: jenidog@gmail.com

WEBSITE: jenimahoney.com

The Monologue:

Tori:

I begged her to go to the clinic, Shell but she just kept saying it was too early, that it wasn't time yet. By the time we're finally on our way - I'm timing the contractions - but they're close. Too close. So I stop to check and I can see: she's coming. But not her head, or her foot - it's like a - I don't know - maybe a shoulder, or a knee - I told her to stop pushing. I begged her, but she wouldn't stop. It was like she was an animal, like she was possessed. And she's pushing and she's screaming at me Shell, begging me to get it out, get it out, get it out. But I can't.

(referring to the baby in her arms:) She's... stuck. Turned wrong, maybe sideways, I can't tell - and there's so much... and it's every where. And I think she must be drowning in there. She must be suffocating, but that's when I see it, Shell. This hand. This precious tiny hand reaching out. For me. For me, Shell. What could I do? There is nothing around us: nothing. Just streams of heat rising up off the road in ribbons and me wishing they would magically turn into something - any thing, any person who could help. And she's begging me, Shell, to get it out get it out get it out - she doesn't care how. She just wants it to be over; wants it out. So I got her out.

True Acting Institute

The Play:

Sweet Fright

The Playwright:

Rex McGregor

Synopsis:

A friendly woman opens the door to a group of trick-or-treaters. She has a special Halloween surprise for them.

About The Playwright:

Rex McGregor is a New Zealand playwright. His short comedies have been produced on four continents from New York and London to Sydney and Chennai. His most popular play, Threatened Panda Fights Back, has had over a dozen productions. Rex has a Master of Arts (Honors) in Languages and Literature from the University of Auckland and is currently a senior collections librarian at Auckland Libraries. Agent: Playmarket: playmarket.org.nz

Contact: rex.mcgregor@xtra.co.nz

Website: rexmcgregor.com

The Monologue:

Donna:

Hello, children. Oooh, what gruesome makeup! I've never seen such hideous witches. You definitely deserve some sweets. But first, may I make a suggestion? When you say "Trick or treat," don't sound so cheerful. Keep in character. Snarl. Cackle. "Trick or treat!" Have a go.

There. Isn't that fun? Scaring the living daylights out of folks. This is my son, Clive. He loves being petrified.

Don't you, darling? Come on. Say hi to the girls.

Please excuse him. He's shy.

80

Clive. Go into the kitchen. Fetch the box. Thanks, darling.

No, no. You didn't frighten him. We're new in the neighborhood. It takes him a while to get used to people. Anyway, this is your lucky night. You've earned much more than a handful of treats. We've got a huge cardboard box for you. Chock-full of sweets. We prepared enough for dozens of children. But only a few groups have knocked on our door. The rest are being careful, I suppose. Avoiding strangers. Even the ones who did knock didn't hang around. You know boys. Scaredy-cats. They ran off without getting so much as a marshmallow. Never mind. All the more for you. It's nearly nine-thirty. So we'll give you the whole lot. Your reward for being big, brave girls. You can dine like queens. For weeks. Sugary delights at every meal. I hope your parents won't mind. I'm terrible. Can't deny Clive anything. He adores soda pops. They're all he drinks. Every day. Our dentist said I should "set limits." I did try. When my darling's teeth first started to rot away, I hid his bottles. But he threw a tantrum. Flailed about on the floor. Banging his precious head. I had to make a decision. What's more important? His mouth or his brain? I gave him the bottles. And followed up with scientific research. Did you know? Every nutrient required for human sustenance can be successfully imbibed through a straw. There's absolutely no need for teeth at all. Or gums. Clive's gums are rotting away now too. Not a pretty sight. But his vital organs are in perfect health. And he's perfectly happy. That's what counts. Here he comes now.

Clive. That's my strong boy. Give the girls the box. And a big smile.

Wait! Girls! Come back! You've left your treats.

There, darling. Wasn't that fun?

THE PLAY:

Birthday Girl

THE PLAYWRIGHT:

Marilyn Millstone

SYNOPSIS:

Julie, 39, dreams of herself as Cinderella. In this monologue, Julie's feisty Fairy Godmother comes to comfort her – sort of.

ABOUT THE PLAYWRIGHT:

Marilyn Millstone is known for writing strong dramatic and comedic roles for women. The semi-historical drama The Sculptress is about the unlikely friendship between a French sculptor in her seventies and a Spanish surrealist painter in her twenties; its world premiere at Fells Point Corner Theatre won two awards from the 2011 Baltimore Playwrights Festival. Her ten-minute comedy Compos Mentis – which is set in a senior living facility and pits a clever elderly lady against a woman forty years her junior – has been produced six times in America and twice abroad; it has won numerous awards. Her ten-minute drama Play Date – about a Muslim woman and a Jewish woman who meet at a bus stop – premiered at the 2018 Rockford New Play Festival (see www.thewssr.org/rockford-new-play-festival-2018/).

In this anthology, the Fairy Godmother monologue is from Birthday Girl, which premiered at the 2018 Silver Spring Stage One-Act Play Festival. Esther's monologue is from Proprioception, a full-length drama that was recently named a winner of AACT NewPlayFest 2020. Proprioception will have its world premiere at Rover Dramawerks in Plano, Texas and will be published in its entirety in an anthology of NewPlayFest winners (see: www.aact. org/newplayfest-2020). Marilyn is currently at work on her first full-length play commission for Prime Stage Theatre in Pittsburgh. She holds an MFA in playwriting from Spalding University.

CONTACT: 240-383-1312

marilynmillstone@hotmail.com (No attachments, please.)

THE MONOLOGUE:

Fairy Godmother:

(THE FAIRY GODMOTHER enters, wearing a ball gown, heels and a glittering tiara and holding the requisite wand. She quickly crosses to the sleeping JULIE, looks down tenderly at her, sighs dramatically, then softly speaks.)

Listen, my dear, you and I have known each other a long time… a really long time. Since you were a little girl. I've enjoyed every moment of it but…I'm afraid I've got some bad news. *(beat)* You know that…thing…that happened to you at the stroke of midnight? The thing every woman in the world secretly dreads? Well…I have to drop you. It's not like I want to, but listen, sweetie, it's like this: I'm the most popular fairy-tale figure in the world. Always have been. I mean, sometimes the wicked witch becomes a temporary fad and takes over but, most of the time, it's me me me, go here, go there, help this girl, help that girl. It's endless, and it's exhausting! I have to draw the line…at age thirty-nine. *(giggling; pleased with herself)* Oh! That rhymes! *(beat)* I love you like a daughter, I truly do. Which is why I have to do what any loving mother should do: I'm kicking you out of the nest. Granting you adulthood. Think of it as a promotion. *(beat)* Oh Julie. I know you dream of yourself as Cinderella, but really, you're a perfectly capable twenty-first century woman…with a weakness for fairy tales. You never needed my help. You're a lovely girl, with a great mind and a kind heart. That's more important than a gown and a tiara and cleavage. Well… I dunno. Cleavage is always *(looking down at her own ample bosom and proudly sighing)* Anyway…All you have to do now is make better choices. I know it's tough being single, childless and…you know…a certain age, but: try not to lose your dignity.

(FAIRY GODMOTHER kisses JULIE on the forehead, and with great flair slowly exits.)

And now, another monologue from Marilyn Millstone

THE PLAY:

Proprioception

SYNOPSIS:

Esther, 89, recounts to a young American woman the story of the day in 1939 when she boarded a kindertransport – a train that took Jewish children out of Nazi Germany to England, where they were placed with sponsoring English families. Esther speaks with a pronounced European accent.

THE MONOLOGUE:

Esther:

The rule was: no drama. Children were to board the train quickly and in an orderly fashion. Once a child boarded, that was it. Parents were not allowed to change their mind. But there was one little girl. Six, I supposed. Maybe seven. Alone, like me. She boarded the train, came into the car I was in. Then a woman – her mother, I supposed – a young girl herself really – began screaming. "No! Shira! My Shira! I cannot let you go!" And she ran onto the train and into our car and bundled the girl in her arms and ran off the train with her. Then a man yanked the girl away from the woman and brought her back into our car. Her father, I guessed. He knelt down and kissed her on each cheek, and on her forehead. Then he left. The little girl didn't cry. She just sat there, looking around. Confused, like the rest of us. Her mother began wailing. "Not my baby! My baby! My baby!" I don't know why I called out to the woman, but I did. "I'll look after her!" I shouted. *(beat)* She looked at me then. Her eyes locked onto mine. She stopped crying. "Do you promise?" she shouted. I looked over at my mother and my bubbe. I saw them nodding. So I took a deep breath and shouted "Yes!" Then someone – I didn't see who – started applauding. And then someone else and someone else and someone else. I didn't know what to do, so I went to the little girl and asked if I could hold her up by the window so her mum and dad could see her, and she said yes, so I picked her up and whispered "Wave and smile," and that is exactly what she did. She waved and smiled and waved and smiled as the train pulled us away from the station. *(beat)* I kept my eyes on my family, of course. The last thing I saw was my father and my grandfather, both standing as tall as they could, doffing their hats to me. And then they disappeared from sight.

THE PLAY:

Queen of Sad Mischance

THE PLAYWRIGHT:

John Minigan

SYNOPSIS:

Shakespeare scholar Beverly Norden, 55, just beginning to be affected by early-onset Alzheimer's, tries to convince her research assistant Kym that the meaning of literature, like the meaning of life, is not determined by its ending.

ABOUT THE PLAYWRIGHT:

John Minigan's work has been produced in the US, Europe, Asia, and Australia and published in the Best American Short Plays, Best Ten-Minute Plays, and New England New Play anthologies. His full-length Queen of Sad Mischance, a 2018 O'Neill Festival Finalist and Dayton FutureFest selection, was developed during the Next Voices Fellowship at the New Repertory Theatre. His full-length comedy Noir Hamlet premiered in Boston in June of 2018 and was a Boston Globe Critics' Pick. He has also developed new work with the Orlando Shakespeare Theater, Actors' Repertory Theatre of Vermont, and the Utah Shakespearean Festival's New American Playwrights Project. John is a member of the Dramatists Guild, StageSource, and the Centastage writers' group.

CONTACT: john.a.minigan@gmail.com, 508 877-3302

WEBSITE: johnminigan.com

THE MONOLOGUE:

Beverly:

Okay. If we can we be serious for a minute. You and I— We both know that at some point, the proteins are going to get so tangled in my brain I won't connect the dots anymore. That's coming. I'm going to wander through the house at night. I'm going to forget who you are—the newest memories go first. I'm going to forget you helped me write the book. I'm going to think you're some stranger, come into my house to take things from me and I may fall into some very ugly thoughts my parents had about people who look like you. That's the pattern of these things, and how a thing ends does not determine what it means.

Yes, cholinesterase inhibitors treat the symptoms. The drugs in the pipeline will do more, but by the time the FDA— If I get them, it'll be too late to make a difference. It'll be when I've managed to lose track of my own name. When I start to choke on my food because I forgot about swallowing. Maybe I won't get the new drugs at all, because a mouthful of chicken salad will have done me in, which will be fine, because even if the drugs do slow this down I'm eventually going to piss myself and— I have to use this plastic mug because I've been misjudging distances and I... I told you that, didn't I? That's where this goes. That's the ending. I'll forget the name of this woman in the painting—what she could have been and how she could have lived—and I'll probably think it's the happiest fucking moment of my life. But it's not, and we know, right now, that it is not. It is ugliness and it is horror... How a thing ends does not determine what it means, and that is why we don't go hang ourselves. Got it?

THE PLAY:

Frozen Masterpieces

THE PLAYWRIGHT:

Elena Naskova

SYNOPSIS:

A young woman with breast cancer says goodbye to her left breast. It's a painful goodbye that ends with a beginning of a new day.

ABOUT THE PLAYWRIGHT:

Elena Naskova is interested in the human condition, and people's struggle to find what's missing and understand what can't be understood.

Elena's plays have been produced and read in Portland, San Luis Obispo, San Francisco, North Hollywood, Chicago, Nantucket, Mesa/Scottsdale, Sheffield - UK, New York, Toronto, Bloomington, Oakland, San Francisco, Madrid – Spain, Dubai, Spokane and Seattle.

Elena is a member of the Dramatist Guild and the Seattle Playwrights Circle.

CONTACT: elenagnaskova@gmail.com, 206-290-6710

WEBSITE: elenagnaskova.wixsite.com/playspp

THE MONOLOGUE:

Valerie:

(Valerie is seated in a chair. Her left breast is painted in bright colors.)

My left breast. My lily. I watched her grow from a tiny, round seed into a flower. I watched her bloom. Minute by minute, hour by hour, day by day. We bloomed together into womanhood. My left breast. My pride. She's me and I'm her. And we were always together. We were together when men's lustful eyes started descending on us.

We were together for our first kiss and caress by a young man's trembling hand. We were together the first time we made love in a cheap motel with a leaky roof. It was raining so hard, there was thunder and from time to time, the black sky would split in two by a penetrating lightning bolt. I bled between my legs for a while and she, she remained hard and erect long after our exhausted lover had fallen asleep. My left breast, she was so alive, so warm, so full and tender. How she used to rest against my cotton shirt. She knew how to wait, how to listen, How to lure, offer, give and take. My left breast, a cushion for my heart. How she raised and descended with every breath I took. How she trembled when my heart was beating fast ... my scarred heart, my tired heart, my sad heart, my wounded heart. My left breast, wrapped in a million sensory nerves, always on alert, waiting, like a riverbed waiting for its river, the river that will never come. Her dormant springs never awakened by a baby's lips. The baby that she and I longed for, for so long.

(gently touches her left breast, as she's looking at it)

How beautiful you are. Painted in warrior colors; ready for the battle that we're doomed to lose. You're trembling but you're not afraid. Right? We're not afraid. What is it that I feel in you? A familiar but forgotten feeling. An energy of desire rushing through you? A desire for a man. A good man. A man with warm hands and hot lips. A man with a set of strong teeth that can bite gently, lovingly, while whispering flattering words, while moaning in ecstasy. *(pause)*

So what are we waiting for, then? Cheer up, my dear. We're going out. We're going to dress up, put on some make-up and go to a bar. Yes, you heard me right? A bar. A bar full of normal people, all dressed up, feeling okay, drinking and talking, looking for someone to go home with. We'll go there and do the same. We'll tell no one about our secret. No one will know and no one will suspect, not for a moment, because we'll smile and look good, we'll smile and laugh, we'll smile and nod, we'll flirt and lure like we've never done it before. Calm down, my dear, this is our night. The night for love. *(pause)*

The night before we part for good.

THE PLAY:

Clarissa

THE PLAYWRIGHT:

Catherine O'Connor

SYNOPSIS:

Who doesn't enjoy a good ghost story? Maybe the ghost.

ABOUT THE PLAYWRIGHT:

Catherine O'Connor is a Washington, DC, based playwright and director. She has directed numerous new play readings and she has participated in the Kennedy Center Page-to-Stage Festival as playwright, director, and producer. Her work has been performed at Theater Alliance, Journeymen Theatre at the Capital Fringe, The Sort-of-Jane-Austen Reading Series of the Washington Shakespeare Company, and the Tavern Stage (DC); Love Creek Productions (NY); the Subversive Theatre Collective (Buffalo, NY); and First Stage (LA). She is a member of the Dramatists Guild.

CONTACT: cocoergo@gmail.com

THE MONOLOGUE:

Clarissa:

(She is pale and her hair is long and stringy. She wears a long, high necked dress. She is young but aged. The setting is the parlor of an old house of indeterminate age. It is dimly lit and the furniture is covered with dusty cloth. There is a window. Clarissa stands by the window. She is holding her hands pressed against the glass.)

No! Children! Please don't run! Listen to me, please. Why do they always run from me? I try to reach out but instead you all flee. I try to push. On doors and windows. I can put my hands up but I have no force. Are you still there? I don't know how I got here. I'm still in Papa's house and I can see my place, the place under the floor where I lie. The baby is there too. I didn't want a baby but what I didn't want didn't matter.

I liked going to school but Papa made me stop. A girl doesn't need school and she doesn't need to see her silly friends. Not when her mother's died and she has to take up the housekeeping and the cooking. And the secret things. The things he told me not to tell. I tried to push back but Papa said I must and I was afraid. This is what a good daughter does when her mother dies. The pastor was supposed to help. He came to talk to me, but then he called me a liar and left angry. Papa made me sorry I said anything.

When the baby was coming, Papa put me in the cellar and told people I had to go to a sanatorium. Later he said I died and I heard the neighbors bringing him food. I could have called out, but I was afraid.

When the baby came I didn't know how to take care of her and she died after a little while. Papa got really angry. He shook me so hard I fell and hit my head. And suddenly I was up by the ceiling and I could see myself on the floor. After a while I heard the neighbors again. This time they were cutting Papa down from the rafter. They found a note that said he couldn't go on because of everything that happened. They all cried and talked about how he had suffered so much.

Now I only hear strangers talk. They come in and laugh and dare each other to spend the night *(To the audience)* You all think it's funny because no one will stay here....Are you there? Can you hear me? Come closer. I have something to tell the children. Push! Be strong...Push back with all your might

THE PLAY:

Backfired

THE PLAYWRIGHT:

Lindsay Partain

SYNOPSIS:

Anna is a high school student who dreams about making the world sparkle; when the boy of her dreams asks to meet her in the cafeteria during geometry, of course she goes! It's going to be winter formal soon, and she's never been kissed before, and —- and absolutely no one could have guessed how this day was going to end.

ABOUT THE PLAYWRIGHT:

Lindsay Partain is an Oregon playwright, an editor for the online literary magazine Cascadia Rising Review, and a member of the Dramatists Guild. She received her B.A. in Theatre from Pacific University in Forest Grove, OR. Recently her work has been produced by the John DeSotelle Studio in New York ("Prayers in the Pines", "Shimmers" & "Dark Horse"), Five & Dime Drama Collective in Arkansas ("Until the Earth Breaks Open"), and was a finalist at the Midwest Dramatist Conference ("Last Dance with MJ"). Her collection of work is available on New Play Exchange.

CONTACT: lgpartain@gmail.com, 971-227-0483

WEBSITE: lindsaypartain.com

THE MONOLOGUE:

Anna:

(16-year old girl in school clothes and a backpack, walks onto a bare stage accompanied only by a ghost light.)

You know the rush you get when you're somewhere you know you shouldn't be? Your heart races and you can feel all of your blood swoosh through your ears and your guts and your fingers? I had snuck into the cafeteria, that's where we were going to meet—me and. Oh, no, hang on— let me go back. I was— I was in Mr. Zukowski's geometry class. Yea, that's right. Math is like, the worst. But there were two bright sides: one. I sit beside my best friend, Liz. Liz is super smart— she wants to be like, a doctor or something. Do you know how long doctors have to go to school for though? Like, another 7 years! And I'm like pffft! As if that's going to happen! We did the career fair together, and Liz went over to all of the different medical booths, but I—, there was these two women, not girls, you could just tell, looking at them. You knew that they were grown, women, with their long blonde hair draped over their shoulders in shiny loose curls like what you see on TV commercials, and their nails were long and thick with that acrylic paint; their booth smelled like Aqua Net hair spray and lavender. That was the day I decided I was going to be a cosmetologist. I wanted to make the whole world sparkle… The world. It's pretty. It's a pretty shitty place.

But. Wait. Where was— right— the second bright side. The second bright side to geometry was Lennon Matthews. He is. He's like. Ohmygod. Lennon is in my study group. The first time I met him he was wearing this really cute grey sweater with the sleeves pushed up so you could see all of the veins on his arms. Like they were just barely being held under his skin.

He passed me a note in Mr. Zukowski's geometry class and asked if I would meet him on the stage in the cafeteria. Winter Formal was coming up, I just— I had a feeling— I was hoping he would ask me, you know? And I was so glad that he picked that day because I was wearing my lucky tenn-ie's and my hair was on. Point. So, I wrote back "yea, when" and he was like "what about now?" and I was like "what do you mean now?" and he was like— "let's go." Like right in the middle of class, he wanted to— just. It was so romantic.

So he left first and after a few minutes I got up and I left too. I opened the double doors to the cafeteria right when a car backfired and I nearly jumped out of my body, but I kept walking. I walked over and up onto the stage at the far end of the cafeteria. I couldn't hear anyone breathing but I could feel their eyes on my skin. I remember I was standing on stage and I was so, weirded out, because it was like I was performing for an audience of ghosts. So, I started searching for Lennon.

"Lennon. Lennon. Where are you?" They think that he was one of the first. They found him in the boy's bathroom. The thick veins that I imagined I might trace from his arms and neck while we slow danced were found flat. You couldn't see the blue of his blood because it painted the mirror and what was left over had drained from his brown skin into the sewage system in the middle of the bathroom floor.

"Lennon? Are you there?" I remember I heard screams coming from the classrooms and then a sharp pop. I don't know why but I tiptoed over to the cafeteria doors to see what was happening and. All I saw was the back of the hat. This like. Rubber, sort of, fishing hat.

Something must have creaked or maybe they could hear the blood drumming in my body, because it was loud enough that I couldn't hear anything else; but they stopped. Like, froze, there in the hallway. They started to turn and that's when I saw the gun. I remember I fell back. Not hard enough to knock the wind out of me but hard enough that it shocked the kick out of my legs and I was crawling like a crab away from the door. Do you remember crawling like a crab when you were little? My whole childhood I'd been practicing walking like a crab when I should have been learning to sprint.

Those double doors that I'd snuck in, minutes before, shot open and slammed against the tile on the walls. I didn't hear the crack but when they swung shut I could see the ceramic had been broken and was falling to the floor in shards. Tears so sharp they cut my arms where they fell. Dark jeans stepping toward me, I heard metal clicking back. Everything was so quiet. The air and everything, so still. Tongue tied— I couldn't beg. Couldn't.

Two things happened then. I thought to myself— this is it. You're going to die. You are going to die never knowing what Lennon Matthews' arms feel like wrapped around your waist. You will never see his reaction when you walk out dressed in sparkles and snow for Winter Formal. The second thing I remember is the warmth. It started in my chest, but that was only blood from where the shotgun peppered me with holes. Before I died, I could feel it working down my legs. I had peed my pants.

And now, another monologue from Lindsay Partain.

The Play:

Curves

Synopsis:

Even the most unapologetically, ferociously confident women have their moments of doubt. When Shayna makes the decision to run off her holiday weight, it opens the door to self-love in the face of god-awful gym culture.

The Monologue:

Shayna:

(Late 20s/early to mid-30s, walks onto the stage and waves at the audience. She is charismatic, a breath of fresh air. She takes a moment, a breath like she's about to get really serious...)

You know how good it feels to finally let go of your stomach? It's a thing, I swear to god. Every woman I know, does this. They suck and they tuck their- oh, yea, I heard it, moving on- we hold in our tummies to make ourselves look skinnier. You know how good it feels for the first like, four seconds after you let go of all of that...belly? But see, the other day I made the mistake of doing this naked. Yea. Fuck me, right? Because no matter how good I feel about myself- no matter how well I eat or how smart I think I am- as soon as I let go of all of that tummy suck- it looks like I gained about 30 pounds. Right before I jump in the shower. Right in front of a mirror. I had seen what I was. What I had become. The kraken had been released. I stood in my shower trying to convince myself that I didn't need to look down to check if I could still see my toes without leaning. That it was just a little weight put on from the holidays. Convincing myself that I wasn't pregnant because you have to have sex to get pregnant and no one really wants to fuck the queen of the trash raccoons who wobbles away from refrigerator flood lights like a sad basset hound.

So what do you do as you step out of the shower looking like you're about to cosplay as Jim Carrey's The Grinch? You all know what I'm thinking. You get yourself….a…say it with me- a gyyyyym—a gym membership- good job. Thank none of you for trying, jesus. So I go to the gym. Wait, hang on, back up. Does anyone here have a membership to a cult- a gym, sorry, anyone? I think we're being screwed. No, seriously, I was calling around to some of these "gyms"—pretty sure that four of the one's that I called were just iron pumping douche bags with a weight set and an elliptical in their mom's basement that wanted to charge me 40 bucks and a good squeeze to use their shady equipment. 40 bucks! And, I know, I know- I don't have to go to a gym. "I could just run outside!" Let me just stop you right there you LuLuLemon Instamodel. Running outside is the actual worst. For one, it's never the right temperature. Mother Nature is always trying to suffocate me with her humidity, or takes a club to my joints with her freezing temperatures, or pelts me in the face with her rain goblins. Also, the impact is terrible on my knees- also- I hate people! When I go for a run, I want to be able to pick and pull at my spandex however the hell I want! When you run fabric goes places you don't want people seeing you remove it from. That made sense. Point being! I had a Grinch belly and I wasn't about to go all house arrest and start doing prison sit-ups in my living room. I make money. I'm getting a gym membership. "But if you don't want people looking at you" mehmehmehemeh I know! I can't fucking win with you guys jesus.

So I got a gym membership and I was all ready to just go in, run on the elliptical because I have the knees of a 90 year-old back alley blow job princess, run for 30 minutes feeling horrible and uncomfortable because other people are forced to be in the same room with me while I run off my turkey shame. But then the woman at the counter said a magnificent thing. "Women's Only Gym".

Do you know who goes to the women's only gym? Women. Older women. I'm talking- Muscle grannies, the women who get off work and go to the gym in a button-down blouse and hit the bike for 5 miles. AKA? Women who don't give a fuck. I looked around at the 4 of us in that room and realized, they don't give a crap about me. They've got problems of their own and they do not give a flying fuck about my turkey weight. They're just happy that I'm not their

15 year old daughter screaming at them because "they had to do the dishes last weekuh". I'm not their recliner husband screaming at them from the living room because they can't find the remote they took 2 seconds to look for. I'm not any of the hundred people asking anything of them and they are not going to spend this precious precious time staring at me and my fat ass.

So what did I do? I ran a few miles- 2, 10-minute miles, no big deal- I lifted a lot of heavy shit with my arms and my legs until I felt all gooey. Then I went home, showered, flexed a little while I dreamed about having a swimmer's body, I got out, stared at myself in the mirror, pinched at my tummy, shrugged, went downstairs and made mac and cheese because I'm a monster. I pretend to notice how many calories are listed on the side but the number means nothing to me so I decide that it must be fine at best and eat the whole box in one sitting. I lay back on my couch with wet hair, a full belly, and shaking legs, and you know what? I feel like a fucking queen. Like, this is the way Beyoncé must feel every night before she goes to bed. It may not have been much and hell it may have only been for me, but damn it— I woke up today feeling good— looking good— and weapons at the ready— that's right, didn't the people tell you at the front? I'm packing heat bitches. I'm armed with killer hips and there's not a single one of you here that's gonna take that from me.

She slaps her ass and lifts her arms at her throwdown like a champion.

THE PLAY:

That Weekend In Belfast

THE PLAYWRIGHT:

Martha Patterson

SYNOPSIS:

Joni remembers a musician who let her down.

ABOUT THE PLAYWRIGHT:

Martha Patterson is a much-produced and oft-published playwright whose plays have been produced in 19 states and eight countries. Her work has been published by the Sheepshead Review, Silver Birch Press, Pioneer Drama Service book, Smith & Kraus / Applause Theatre & Cinema Books, and the Afro-Hispanic Review. She has a B.A. from Mt. Holyoke and an M.A. from Emerson College. She lives in Boston, Massachusetts, the USA.

CONTACT: MPatterson125933@aol.com

WEBSITE: marthapatterson.org

THE MONOLOGUE:

Joni:

(Talking to an unseen friend about a man who treated her to a day at a music festival. Drinking a shot of whisky.)

Oh, listen, I've been with musicians…for a long time they were the only types I'd date. There was Sam. Sam played guitar in a band, The Burning Skeletons, and I thought maybe I could land a free ticket to a festival if I went out with him, right? Well, I did – at Titanic Slipways. Because Belfast needs music, not just political conflict, right? Dyed my hair green and partied my life out that weekend. Sedated by lots of booze. But Sam liked dressing in women's clothes. I found out, not the first night, but the second night I spent with him, because after the festival, we got stoned together and went to bed.

But it was like an acid trip. Dressed up in garters and a corset, he was, and he had the nerve to ask if I fancied it. Fancied it? I was appalled! No man I'd spent the night with did that before. And this was after he'd set fire to his guitar onstage! Which really turned me on. But then – the transvestite business. Sam wasn't queer, not that there's anything wrong with that – he just liked getting in touch with the "female" side of himself. Maybe 'cuz his Mum took off for Galway when he was only three and he was raised by his Dad. Such a disappointment, he was, after a day of musical bliss. Well, if I wanted to go to bed with someone dressed like a lady, I'd go out with a lady, for Heaven's sake! But I'm not cut out of that kind of cloth. Anyway, at least I had a wild weekend in Belfast to show for it. And The Burning Skeletons were brill.

THE PLAY:

Supergirls! Tales of Life, Love, and Captain Nebraska

THE PLAYWRIGHT:

Amanda Petefish-Schrag

SYNOPSIS:

The Harrier, a former superhero with the power to invade people's minds, never intended to become a supervillain, and yet... Here she describes her first attempt to leave Nebraska and the beginning of her journey to infamy.

ABOUT THE PLAYWRIGHT:

Amanda Petefish-Schrag is an Assistant Professor of Theatre at Iowa State University. Her professional credits include work as a playwright, puppeteer, director, actor, and mom. Her playwriting work has been produced at festivals and theaters in London, Chicago, New York, Los Angeles, Kansas City, Minneapolis, Milwaukee, and Iowa City, and has been published by Playscripts, Inc., and Smith and Kraus. In 2017 she was a Br!nk Playwright in Residence at Renaissance Theatre Works in Milwaukee, Wisconsin. Amanda is a member of the Dramatists Guild, the International Union of Marionette Artists, the Puppeteers of America, and is a past recipient of the Kennedy Center National Teaching Artist Grant and the Missouri Governor's Award for Excellence in Higher Education.

CONTACT: petefishschrag@gmail.com, 515-203-7818

WEBSITE: newplayexchange.org/users/20798/amanda-petefish-schrag

THE MONOLOGUE:

The Harrier:

I loved New York. The sheer humanity of the city, the cacophony of sound . . . of thought. It's beautiful and – horrifying. My mother only got the horror. My mother: A quintessential fifth generation pioneer – strong, smart, charitable, and always waiting for the natives to attack. She used to call every Sunday to tell me "the news" - girls who got stabbed on the subway, or contracted hepatitis from sweaty night club dancers. Or about her friend's daughter's roommate's cousin who got mugged on her way to church. I told her not to worry. I promised to always use the buddy system, and never ride the subway after dark. *(Beat.)*

I never use the buddy system and frequently rode the subway after dark, but since I could cause someone to have a nervous breakdown with a quick "flip of the brain," I really didn't worry about muggers. Or anyone. Certainly not the cute guy in my Stats class who asks me out one Friday night in November. The guy who pays for my dinner and thinks that entitles him to more than interesting conversation. And through the whole – incident - I don't do anything. Because I am drunk. And because I am scared. Terrified.

Fear: A distressing emotion aroused by impending danger, evil, or pain, whether the perceived threat is real or imagined. Captain Nebraska says our power is instinctual. He's wrong. Fear is instinctual. Power is the choice we make in the face of fear.

At the end of our "date" Stats Man kisses me. He kisses me and walks home. And I watch him go. I could have made him run in front of an oncoming car. I could have made him trip on the stairs. I could have made him wet his pants. But I just watched him go. *(Beat.)* I moved back to Nebraska a week later.

THE PLAY:

Welcome To Keene, NH

THE PLAYWRIGHT:

Brian James Polak

SYNOPSIS:

Mrs. Cunningham was married to Mr. Cunningham for 60+ years and they lived their entire lives in the same small town where they met. This monologue occurs at the beginning of the final act of the play; Mrs. Cunningham died at the end of the previous act.

ABOUT THE PLAYWRIGHT:

Brian James Polak is a New Hampshire playwright currently residing in Chicago. He has been awarded The Kennedy Center's Jean Kennedy Smith Award and John Cauble Award, an Eliot Norton Award, and 4th place in the 1985 Chesterfield School spelling bee. Several of his one-acts have been published in Smith & Kraus "Best of…" anthologies. Brian produces and hosts American Theatre Magazine's THE SUBTEXT podcast where he interviews playwrights about their lives and their work. He received his MFA in Dramatic Writing from The USC School of Dramatic Arts.

CONTACT: BrianJamesPolak@gmail.com

WEBSITE: BrianJamesPolak.com

THE MONOLOGUE:

Mrs. Cunningham:

I was married to Mr. Cunningham for over sixty years. That's a long time. Longer than some people even get to live. We married in 1957. I was nineteen years old. He was twenty-one. It was a nice ceremony. Both of our families were there. You could say it was traditional. White dress. All that business.

I enjoyed being married… being a wife. It wasn't always easy. I know everybody says that…. because it's true. Being married is hard. I can't say I ever wanted to not be married to Mr. Cunningham, but we had our share of disagreements. Some of them rising to the level of argument. Sometimes it was over serious issues. Sometimes it was over politics. Mr. Cunningham voted for Richard Nixon. Twice. We somehow managed to get through that. I'm proud to say, after many years of wearing him down, I got him to vote for a Democrat. Twice. We often struggled to pay proper attention to each other. We'd get caught up in whatever it was we had swimming in our own heads.

It's hard when things don't seem to go your way. You want your person to know what you're feeling without you having to tell them. You want them to know what to do without having to ask. But that's not how people work. You must have dedication to the people around you. You've got to really see them. Not simply look, but see. There were times when I wanted to scream "Look at me! I'm standing right here!" But I'd say nothing. I'd go into the bedroom and cry for eight minutes. Then I'd be okay again.

When I got sick… those last two years got really bad for me… he never complained. We became more connected than ever before. It was a wonderful time for us. I mean, despite the fact that I was dying. He saw me. And I saw him. It took many years to get there, but it happened. And I'm so glad it did.

If I could give any advice to people today, I'd say… We all need. And we all can give. That's what makes us human. Give and take in as equal measure as you can.

THE PLAY:

At the Barre

THE PLAYWRIGHT:

Yasmine Beverly Rana

SYNOPSIS:

Elizabeth, an ethereal ballet student in her fifties, stands at the barre to celebrate her return to dance following her bout with cancer.

ABOUT THE PLAYWRIGHT:

Yasmine Beverly Rana's numerous publications include The War Zone is My Bed and Other Plays, an anthology of four of Rana's plays published by Seagull Books and University of Chicago Press. World Premieres include La MaMa Experimental Theatre (The War Zone is My Bed), The Looking Glass Theatre (Blood Sky), Johns Hopkins University Theatre (Returning), Nora's Playhouse (The Fallen) among others. Awards include a New Jersey State Council on the Arts fellowship for playwriting (Another Spring).

CONTACT: Susan Gurman Agency

assistant@gurmanagency.com, 212-749-4618

THE MONOLOGUE:

Elizabeth:

(A center barre in a ballet studio in New York City. Elizabeth, an ethereal woman in her fifties, stands at the front barre. Speaks to audience.)

It doesn't feel different. I mean, it is different, aesthetically, physically, biologically, different, but it doesn't feel different to me *(Hand over breast)*. Okay, the balance is off a little (Attempts to pirouette), okay more than a little but, I'm still here *(Grips the barre)*. I guess I shouldn't be here according to the research. Perhaps I shouldn't be here because I make others uncomfortable. But I was a dancer, albeit not a very famous one, but I worked with small companies, at times, so I should, could say I was a real dancer who used to love my body. Who loves their bodies? I did. I loved the way it felt and the way it moved. Others loved it too. But not anymore. Who wants this? I couldn't wait to return. In the hospital, in rehab, in treatment, I would yearn for the moment to return to the barre. I even recalled and regretted those few days when I was well and whole, and skipped class because the weather was too beautiful to be indoors or I had a better offer, usually comprised of two drinks before sex with some random someone. That was better, than this *(Acknowledging barre)*? Unsatisfying sex is never better than this. I couldn't wait to return and I had after the third, no fourth surgery and reconstruction, I would change in the dressing room with everyone else. Why not? It had never occurred to me to do anything different. My body for months, years had become … hollow, an object, an experimental instrument, a variable in the equation, so distant from my soul, that I even questioned if I had kept my soul, "Had it been cut out with everything else?" And if it had been removed, and if I had become this … passive variable, having everything "done" to me outside of my control, undressing in front of others would seem, invisible. But it wasn't, because I wasn't invisible, but a reminder to other women, and their bodies, young and old that they too could become me. I think some even feared of coming too close to me, not out of fear of contagion, but some sort of osmosis that this *(Acknowledging her body)* instrument, was a body, the body they exercise at the barre, the body they stretch and contort and lift and balance and unbalance and hate and maybe *(Reflects)* love. This body could be their body. It's mine now but it could be someone else's tomorrow. Please don't think I wish *(Acknowledging her body)* this on anyone. *(Resolutely)* Because I don't. If I saw someone in the dressing room who was a reflection of me, I too would be *(Searching)* uncomfortable, scared. I don't mind changing in the bathroom stall. It's fine, claustrophobic and unsanitary, but fine. I don't mind it as long as I can still be here and move, not as … effortlessly as I had moved before or as gracefully or as youthfully or as … naively, but as me, now, as what I have become, what I am.

> *(Elizabeth steps away from the barre. She slowly, slightly painfully raises her arms and bends to her knees in supplication.)*

THE PLAY:

Homeschooled

THE PLAYWRIGHT:

Kristin Kay Rasmussen

SYNOPSIS:

Overachieving Alissa has had everything go wrong on her way to a scholarship interview at a prestigious university. When she finally makes it to her meeting, the committee repeatedly questions the merits of her education because she has been homeschooled her entire life.

ABOUT THE PLAYWRIGHT:

Kristin Kay Rasmussen studied theater at Michigan State University. She is now an educator and playwright living in Michigan. Her monologues and sketches have been published by Lillenas Drama and in the monologue collection "My Side of the Story." She has also had her work produced at the Forward Theater Company as part of their monologue festivals.

CONTACT: kriskrasmussen@gmail.com

WEBSITE: krisrasmussen.net

THE MONOLOGUE:

Alissa:

(melting down just a little in frustration, Alissa makes one last case for why she is a superior candidate.)

Yes, I have been homeschooled my entire life, though I prefer the term independently educated. Independently educated doesn't tend to conjure up images of socially awkward, poorly dressed children who are being raised in a military bunker or in some type of commune. My SAT score is 1350. I have passed three advanced placement courses. I didn't accomplish all of that by calling a walk in the backyard my science project. I speak two other languages because I have gone on missions trips since I was five. Hablo dos idiomas español y francés *(Beat)* Je suis plus intelligent que toi.

(deep breath)

Yes, I do have a slight obsession with "Little House on the Prairie", but should that really be held against me? If you understood the progressive political ideals of Laura Ingalls Wilder, so would you. I can stop bingewatching the series every Thanksgiving…and Christmas…. and on her birthday… any time I want. I can. The bottom line is this. I am an independent thinker because my school experience was not formed by being locked in a room six hours a day having to ask someone else when I can pee. I haven't been trained by a bell to move from here to there. And when was the last time you had a scholarship candidate in your office who could look you in the eye, carry on a conversation and not feel anxiety because he or she wasn't able to text somebody for five mnutes? *(beat)* Exactly. Any other questions?

THE PLAY:

The Cody Monologues: Famous and Infamous Women of the West

THE PLAYWRIGHT:

Bethany Hamilton Sandvik

SYNOPSIS:

Caroline Lockhart was an unapologetic author who told the truth as she saw it. Best known for her book, "The Lady Doc," written in 1912, Lockhart loved to poke fun at prominent members of society in her articles and stories and was not afraid to call them out on issues she disagreed with. In this monologue, Caroline explains why she is the way she is. Lockhart was inducted into the Cowgirl Hall of Fame in October 2018.

ABOUT THE PLAYWRIGHT:

Bethany Hamilton Sandvik is the Founder and Director of Studio Theatre at CCPA. Her play, The Cody Monologues: Famous and Infamous Women of the West won a 2017 "Honorable Mention" in Fine Arts from the Wyoming Historical Society and has been running each summer since 2016 at the Studio Theatre in Cody, Wyoming. She also serves as Marketing Director and a dance instructor at the Cody Center for the Performing Arts. Sandvik received a BA in Communications/Theatre from Allegheny College and an MS in Arts Management from Drexel University.

Sandvik produced, acted, directed, and wrote professionally for the stage in both Cleveland and Philadelphia. She was a two-time participant of the Theatre in Museums national conference at the Indianapolis Children's Museum and has helped write and direct several devised theatre pieces for the Cody High School drama team. Sandvik lives in Cody, Wyoming with her husband Jeff and their two children, Jacob and Beatrice.

CONTACT: bethanysandvik@gmail.com, 307.527.7398

WEBSITE: studiotheatreccpa.org

THE MONOLOGUE:

Caroline:

I was born in Illinois but was raised in Kansas, just outside of Topeka. I learned to ride a horse and cuss like a ranch hand at a very young age. I drove my mother to distraction. She once told me, "Caddie, if you don't stop cussin' and carrying on, God will send a bolt of lightning to strike you down ——-God is ALWAYS watching." Well, I'll be honest. It did frighten me some. But even at the age of 5, I was someone who wanted to know and experience the truth. So, I got my little brother George, we walked out in the yard, looked up at the clouds and after taking a deep breath yelled to the heavens, "Go to Hell, God-dammit." We waited for a while, and after nothing happened, George and I realized we could pretty much get away with anything....I've sorta lived that way ever since.

Mama died when I was a girl and after being practically raised by a "painted lady" in our town, it was suggested I go back East to finishing school, so I could get lessons on becoming a proper lady. *(Smile)*. As you can imagine, it didn't go well.

THE PLAY:

Becky and the Magic Harp

THE PLAYWRIGHT:

David Skeele

SYNOPSIS:

A socially stunted daycare worker turns her life of sexual repression and confusion into a fairy-tale allegory for her group of preschoolers.

ABOUT THE PLAYWRIGHT:

David Skeele teaches acting and playwriting, and has directed over forty shows at Slippery Rock University. David's original plays have received professional and collegiate productions in Los Angeles, Pittsburgh, Cleveland, Columbus, Omaha, and Orlando and internationally in Switzerland, Australia, England, Canada and Nigeria. In recent years, a number of David's plays—The Barwell Prophecy, Dark North, Hungry Jane, The Margins, Deepchurch Hollow, and Electra: An American Gothic—have premiered at Edinburgh Festival Fringe in Edinburgh, Scotland, where they have received coveted five-star reviews. His horror novel Raised In Darkness is available on amazon.com.

CONTACT: david.skeele@sru.edu

THE MONOLOGUE:

Becky:

(An attractive, if slightly dowdy woman in her late twenties. She stands in front of a group of unseen children. She is distraught, and is attempting to gather herself together, to keep the same cheery outlook that she presents to the kids every other day. There is something wide-eyed and babyish about her way of speaking and acting—the result of spending her entire life working with young children. There is, perhaps,

though, the sense of some other kind of awareness trying to break through the child-like surface.)

Okay, people! People! People, please put on your listening ears now. Listening ears, that's right. I wanted to say something to you. I wanted to say I'm sorry. I apologize for crying out there. And for cutting your outside time short. Yes, I'm fine now. Really. No, Mackenzie, it wasn't you. I promise. No, Tyler, it wasn't you, either. Are you crying, Tyler? It wasn't you! It wasn't any of you. Please don't cry. Hey, I have an idea. Story time! Yes, how would that be? An extra-special, super-duper morning-time version of afternoon story time! *(Starts to cry.)*

Stop it now, or you're going to make me do it again. All right? Let's do the wipe-away, okay? Everybody put on your saddest expression. Sad, sad. Sad faces. No, Max, that just looks...scary. Sad, okay? Ready? Now, wipe it away.

(She puts her hands on her forehead and "wipes" downward, leaving a happy expression.)

That's it. Wipe. Okay. Isn't that better? All right, then. All ready for story time? You don't look all ready. What are you missing? That's right, Sarah: hand-hugs and pretzel-feet. Hand-hugs and pretzel feet, every body! Mackenzie, Robinson, McCallister—those don't look like pretzel feet, do they? Do they? All right, then. Thank you. Ashford! Ashford! I appreciate that you want to show affection for Sarah, but while we are in day-care we are keeping our bodies to ourselves, aren't we? Yes, you may pat her arm, lightly, if Sarah doesn't mind. Ask permission, please. Ashford? All right, thank you, Sarah. That's right, Ashford. Lightly. Yes, like that.

(She watches for a long moment, pasting on a patient smile)

Okay. Are you finished? Then—hand-hugs. Thank you. So. Story time. Okay, let's see...

(She takes a deep breath)

So. Once upon a time, it seems there was...

(She makes a decision)

...A princess... That's right, a princess. Yes. McFadden? No, there is no book today. Yes, that's very true, but stories don't always come from books. Well, they come from our…brains and our hearts. Okay? Well, once upon a… Yes, Robinson? Yes, I'm sure the class would be very interested in hearing about the brain you saw, but right now I am speaking. Right now I am attempting to tell you a story, and the appropriate, respectful thing to do would be to put your hands back in a nice little hug and listen. Okay?

Once there was a princess named…named…well, actually she didn't have a name. That's right. She didn't have a name. She… No, she was just a princess. She didn't… Yes, Mackenzie, Princess Mackenzie is a very nice name, but it isn't this princess' name… Wait. People. People. She didn't have a name!! All right?

Okay. This nameless, no-name Princess. She lived in her…castle. A small castle, but it was hers. And…her whole life she had owned a precious possession. It was a…harp. A small harp. And she had always been taught by her mother—the Queen—to keep the harp to herself, and never show it to anyone, or…let anyone play it.

What, Max? No, it wasn't made of gold. And that's a very good question, sweetie, because in fact…the harp was…not pretty. It was made of…wood and…stone and… No, not stone. I don't know, but the Princess, you see, even though she thought it was her most precious possession, the Princess didn't really even think that someone else would ever like the harp.

So, she kept the harp…up on a high, high shelf in her castle room. With her beanie babies and all her friendship bracelets from 2009 to 2014. Up where she couldn't see it, and she wouldn't think about it. Even though she did still think about it. A lot.

Now, there were a few princes—not many, but a few—who came to the princess and wanted to see the harp. And she liked some of these princes, she really did. Well, one of them was really nice, anyway. But…they all wanted to see the harp, and even though part of her wanted to show it to them, an even bigger part of her was scared to show it to them. Because it was too precious, and… if something happened to the harp then she…she…well, she didn't know what would happen to her.

Yes, Tyler? Yes, that's right. That's exactly what it was—a magic harp, and…well, it seems—she believed this, anyway—that the

Queen had put a spell on her when she was very little. That's right, a spell, a terrible spell. And the spell was...that if something happened to the harp—if anything happened to the harp—the Princess wouldn't be special anymore. She wouldn't be anything.

And also she was scared that the princes wouldn't like the harp, and that maybe they were only being nice to her so she would let them see the harp, and play on the harp, and if they saw the harp and didn't like it then they wouldn't want to be nice to her anymore.

So she...kept the harp high on its shelf, and the princes... Well, they went away. All of them, eventually. Which told the Princess that she had been right all along. They only wanted the harp, and without the harp they didn't really care about the Princess. Even the really nice prince.

But she couldn't ever really stop thinking about the stupid harp. I mean, the magic harp. Hand-hugs! Hand-hugs, McAllister! Jacob! What? No, it's not a boring story. It's not a boring story, and any inside time we spend complaining or squirming or demonstrating inappropriate behavior will be taken out of our outside time. Do we want that? No, we do not. Yes, Ashford. Thank you, Ashford. I don't think it's a boring story, either.

All right. Now, here is the thing. She had also heard something very bad about harps—about her harp. She'd heard some women on T.V.—um, wise women of...royal T.V.—say that if you don't... that if she didn't...play on her harp, that if she never showed it to anyone, that...well, that it would do terrible things to her brain. I don't know what things, Robinson. I don't know what kind of things, except that she would...slowly go crazy. She would be a crazy, ugly old Princess, alone in her castle with her cold, dusty harp.

Then, one day a new prince came along. And he wasn't necessarily the most handsome prince, or the nicest prince, but he didn't seem to care that the Princess was old. And he began to take the Princess to dinner at various, expensive places around the...kingdom, and even though he wasn't the handsomest or the nicest prince the Princess had met, she's thinking she should just go ahead and let him play the stupid thing and get it over with. And in fact she decided that was what she was going to do, but then a friend of hers told her that this prince, in fact, is also married to a different princess in a different castle.

Yes, McAllister, that can happen. Yes, it is possible. It happens all the time. Apparently.

(She begins to struggle with tears again.)

So. What was the Princess to do? The prince came to see her in her castle, and she had so many decisions to make and she was angry and sad and lonely and confused and finally she just said... what the heck. (Pause.)

She...unveiled the harp. Let him play it.

What, McFadden? What did it sound like? What...a wonderful question. What did it sound like. It didn't really...sound like anything. She just lay there, listening for something, but... And then, when he was finished playing it, he left. It was just as she'd feared. He didn't like the harp. Or, once he had the harp, he had no reason to see the Princess anymore...

Yes, Tyler? Yes, that is the ending. Yes. It is a terrible ending, isn't it? What if...the Princess threw herself into the moat? That's what she does. Wouldn't that be better?

(Looks around her, startled.)

Okay. Okay. She doesn't have to do that. I'm sorry. Please don't cry, Mackenzie. She won't throw herself in the moat. But...I just don't know what else she should do. What...? Robinson? Hmm. If she killed the Queen, would it lift the spell? Yes. Yes, I think it would. But it wouldn't be very nice. MacAllister? Find another Princess to be her friend. Well... That is a thought.

Max? Wait, people. Max was saying something. What, Max? She should get a guitar. Well, I don't know if that would... I'm sorry, an electric guitar.

(Thinks about it. A revelation.)

Yes, you know what, Max? That's exactly what she did. She threw that old harp away and she...started over again, with a shiny new electric guitar. And she never told the Queen anything about it. And...she threw away all her beanie babies and her friendship bracelets and…okay, no—she gave away the beanie babies, to all her dear, little friends. And then she left her little friends, and moved far away where no one knew her, and learned to play her guitar. And one day, she learned how to make the loudest, most beautiful music anyone had ever heard.

The end.

Go on. I see Miss Ashleigh coming. Go on out. She'll let you play outside. Go on. That's right. Go. *(She kneels, talking to an invisible child.)*

What, Ashford? Yes. Yes, I think it's a really good story, too.

(She kisses him.)

Goodbye.

(She watches the children leave.)

THE PLAY:

Bee Trapped Inside The Window

THE PLAYWRIGHT:

Saviana Stanescu

SYNOPSIS:

May is a foreign domestic worker, an undocumented immigrant in the US, trapped in a domestic slavery situation in the suburbs of CT. The monologue details her daily life as a list of tiring domestic tasks.

ABOUT THE PLAYWRIGHT:

Saviana Stanescu is an award-winning Romanian-American playwright, scholar, and ARTivist based in New York/Ithaca. Her plays have been produced around the world. Her US plays include Aliens with extraordinary skills, Ants (both published by Samuel French), Bee Trapped Inside the Window, Lenin's Shoe, Useless, For a Barbarian Woman, Toys, Bechnya, Hurt (Best American Short Plays 2012), Waxing West (2007 NY Innovative Theatre Award), developed/produced by Women's Project, New York Theatre Workshop, La MaMa Theatre, EST, New Georges, Lark, Cherry, Teatro La Capilla, Teatrul Odeon, etc. Saviana's Romanian plays include Inflatable Apocalypse (2000 UNITER Award), Medea Bar, Infanta. Users' Guide, Final Countdown. She holds an MA in Performance Studies and an MFA in Dramatic Writing from New York University. She is an Associate Professor of Playwriting and Contemporary Theatre at Ithaca College.

WEBSITE: saviana.com

THE MONOLOGUE:

May:

5 am – Wake up.

Cold floor. Barefoot. Door squeaks.

Quiet. No wake up kids.

Go kitchen. Clean sink.

Missus always gets mad if the sink is dirty.

Make eggs. Warm milk.

6 am – Wake kids.

Wash kids. Wash ears, wash neck.

Toast bread. Cereals. Captain Crunch.

Spill milk. Little Johnny cry.

Shhhh. No wake missus.

Wipe table.

Kids eat. Hate me.

Say: "stupid"!

I'm no stupid.

Call me "May - do this, do that"

"May" not my name.

Help kids dress.

T-shirt. Jeans. Socks. Shoes.

Backpack. Ready.

Bus comes. Kids go.

7 am - Clean sink.

Missus always gets mad if the sink is dirty.

Let dog Sparky out.

Fresh morning air.

    (enjoying the fresh air)

Goood.

Enough. Hurry. Back.

7.30 am - Wake Missus and Mister.

Make breakfast. OMELETTE.

Spinach, cheese, for Missus.

Ham, peppers, for Mister.

Missus yells. Sink no clean!

Oh no. Little piece of pepper there.

Coffee. Mister spills. Missus mad.

They argue.

More coffee.

9 am - Missus and Mister leave.

Clean sink.

Start laundry.

To garage. Wash car.

Vacuum living room, hallway, kids room.

4 bathrooms. No gloves.

Clean toilet. Sink.

Scrub floor. Get corners.

Missus always checks corners.

Finish laundry.

Start iron.

Don't forget to change

Toilet paper.

1 pm – Kids back.

Make lunch. Clean kitchen.

Put kids sleep nap.

Finish iron.

Go out. Fresh air. Gooood.

Flowers. Bees. Butterflies.

Nice colors.

Hurry. Clip bushes.

Kids wake. Want snack.

Make sandwich.

Clean sink. Clean table.

Kids play living room.

Kids make mess living room.

6 pm – Missus and Mister back.

Stickers. Nice colors.

Mister throws stickers in garbage.

They argue.

Clean living room.

Cook dinner.

Clean kitchen. Oven. Floor. Sink.

Missus always gets mad if the sink is dirty.

Take garbage out.

Save stickers. Nice colors.

Set table. Bring food.

Sauce pasta no good.

Missus angry.

Make new sauce.

Family eat. I serve.

Clean kitchen. Oven. Floor. Sink.

Missus always gets mad if the sink is dirty.

Take dog Sparky out.

Fresh air.

Good.

Hurry.

9 pm – Kids go bed. Not yet.

More iron.

Bath for missus.

Help missus hair dry.

Rub missus feet.

10 pm – Missus and Mister go bedrooms.

Not yet.

Family watch TV.

They argue.

Clean living room. Not yet.

Kids want milk and snack.

Make sandwich.

Missus wants glass of wine.

Bring glass of wine.

"Not red, white!"

Bring white wine.

Mister wants whisky.

Bring whisky.

"Not good for your stomach!"

They argue.

11 pm – Put kids sleep.

Missus and Mister go bedrooms.

Sex? *(listens to what happens upstairs)*

Wash sheet tomorrow?

No. They argue.

Midnight - They sleep.

Clean downstairs.

Living room. Kitchen. Sink.

Missus always gets mad if the sink is dirty.

Shhhh. Don't make noise.

1 am – Finish clean.

Look stickers.

Oh no, colors dirty.

I'm dirty.

I want to take bath.

No, can't. They hear.

I wash my armpits.

I wash my neck.

I wash my face.

I wash my hands.

I put my foot in the sink. Wash.

I put the other foot in the sink. Wash.

Missus always gets mad if the sink is dirty.

2 am – Go sleep.

Don't dream.

THE PLAY:

Naming True

THE PLAYWRIGHT:

Natalie Symons

SYNOPSIS:

Terminally ill Nell Jordan, who spent her life on the streets of Detroit, comes to Hill's Lodge Motel in the Florida Panhandle with her cat T.S. to finish her childhood memoir about her brother True, who is incarcerated for killing the man that abused them as children. Amy, a transgender teenage girl shows up unannounced with hopes of rescuing Nell.

ABOUT THE PLAYWRIGHT:

Natalie Symons' plays have been developed and produced at theatres around the country, including ACT Theatre, Aurora Theatre, American Stage, freeFall Theatre, New American Theatre, Theater Schmeater, Florida Studio Theatre, Bridge Street Theatre, Theatre22, Amas Musical Theatre, New Century Theatre, and Urbanite Theatre.

Natalie is the playwright-in-residence at American Stage. She is the author of the upcoming novel LIES IN BONE. NAMING TRUE premiered at Urbanite Theatre and is available as an on-demand podcast at Ashland New Play Festival's play4keeps.org.

CONTACT: nataliesymons.author@gmail.com

WEBSITE: nataliesymons.com

THE MONOLOGUE:

Nell:

What's you sorry about? I don't need you to be sorry for me. *(A little laugh.)* Oh baby girl, I've slept in shelters, jail cells, and in the dirty stinking gutter. And them is just some of the fancier spots. *(Off AMY's look.)* So stop looking down your nose at me. Your life ain't been so rosy either kid. Yours pretty much sucked before you even come out. You were born with the wrong parts for Christ sake. If you ask me, that's something to be pissed off about, but you ain't complaining. And neither am I. So don't you be hurling your judgments at me girly. Only God does the judging. People called me every form of every awful thing, while I just been looking for something to eat or a place to shit or sleep. When you been invisible long as me and True have, sooner or later you end up in some hole - some rat-hole, dope-hole, or shit-hole. So my brother is in his hole. And I'm here in mine - next door to that bible-thumpin' raisin - where I drink, I type, and I bleed. *(Taking a nip of whiskey.)* Now that I'm done typing, all that's left is the drinking and the bleeding. All you folks making apologies like I'm some kind of tragedy. Wanting to shine me up nice and pretty - you people is the worst of all. That white raisin Wanda-in-eleven tries to shine me up. Gets all up in my shit with her bible rant. Kept coming over here with those five teeth - saying she's here to give T.S. catnip and then shoving her stinky old bible in my face, calling it the good book. I told her she was welcome to think it's a good book - but I ain't read it so I'll make up my own damn mind if it's a good book or not. "I worry about your soul Miss Nell. I pray for you." Like I'm some kind of charity case. That white bitch has five fuckin' teeth stickin' out of her gums. Only got a couple hairs left on her head, and she lives in a goddamn roach-infested motel room - and she's lookin' down her nose at me? T.S. wasn't having it. She squirt a little pee on that bitch. *(A laugh.)* Told her T.S. didn't mean no harm. "She just wanted to leave a little something for you to remember her by Miss Wanda." *(A laugh.)* Old Wanda-in-eleven ain't come back since. *(Pause.)* Only one person in my life ever shined me up where I didn't feel like a dope. *(Reverently.)* Little east side girl named Susan. An angel in a waste land. She and her daddy didn't have a pot to piss in or a window to throw it out of, but she took me and True in and shined us up all nice. *(Off AMY's look.)* Why you keep staring at me with them eyes like that?

THE PLAY:

Here, Somewhere

THE PLAYWRIGHT:

Rebecca VerNooy

SYNOPSIS:

Tina, a college aged young woman, has come off her meds. She is manic, and speaking to a friend. Her newfound freedom and optimism are palpable (if not sustainable).

ABOUT THE PLAYWRIGHT:

Rebecca VerNooy is a movement theatre artist, actress and writer. Her original work has been produced at Dixon Place, P.S. 122, Judson Church, Ensemble Studio Theatre, Dance Theatre workshop, and Joyce Soho. Her essay, Authentic Movement and its Application to Contemporary Performance Training, was published in the anthology, Movement for Actors II (Allworth Press). She is working on her first book, Both Sides of Crazy, a memoir about chaos and Mindfulness.

Rebecca is the founder of The Movement Educator's Research Group (MERGE), a collaborative research group for movement educators across the country. She has taught Movement, Acting, Physical Theater and Mindfulness at Ensemble Studio Theater, Caymichael Patten Studio, The School for Film and Television, New York Film Academy, Hampshire College and Rutgers University. She is currently a faculty member at Ohio University's School of Theatre, Director of Education for Tantrum Theatre and a freelance creative consultant.

CONTACT: Rebecca@rebeccavernooy.com

THE MONOLOGUE:

Tina:

I am a star. I am a star. I am a star. I dance. I radiate. I shine the light upon the world. That's how I feel. Like I will last forever. Well, stars don't last forever, but they live a long, long life. All of that energy. I feel like I could run a marathon. All of that light. I banish the darkness! I have finally conquered that hell. What are we but the stuff of stars? My blood is the ocean. My heart is the sun. My bones are the trees. And my brain…it's just… mud. Ah, that was so bad. But it's true. I feel it. In my bones. In my blood. Through my eyes. Alive and free from this torture *she taps her head.*

I know this feeling will pass, but I can remember it. It's the forgetting that's the problem, the culprit, the oppressor. Why can't I remember this feeling? We have built in forgetters that blind us from the truth. And the truth is that we are brilliant.

How can I remember? This is who I really am. It's like the masks have peeled away. *As she peels across her face.* Bye-bye high school mask. *Across heart/ribs.* Bye fear mask. *As if taking off a dress.* Bye dainty, girlie. *She dances around making sounds of joy.* I am a star. I am the light. I don't need those meds!!

A revelation. Matter of fact I will not collapse, but shoot through the sky toward a dynamic death. *She laughs.* I'm not suicidal, not today. That was just a metaphor. I'm going to remember this—how I feel. I am. I am. Yah!

THE PLAY:

Church & State

THE PLAYWRIGHT:

Jason Odell Williams

SYNOPSIS:

Three days before his bid for reelection, in the wake of a school shooting in his hometown of Raleigh, North Carolina, a Republican U.S. senator makes an off-the-cuff comment to a blogger that gets leaked on "the Twitter," calling into question the senator's stance on guns and God. In this monologue, the senator's devoutly Christian wife, Sara, tries to convince her husband not to change the stump speech he is scheduled to deliver to a packed crowd of over 800 people in just a few minutes.

ABOUT THE PLAYWRIGHT:

Jason Odell Williams is an award-winning playwright as well as an Emmy-nominated writer and producer. OFF-BROADWAY: Church & State, New World Stages (Best New Play Nominee – Off-Broadway Alliance and L.A. Ovation Awards, NNPN Rolling World Premiere); Handle With Care, Westside Theatre (NY Times Critics' Pick; WINNER, Outstanding Production, Theatre Bay Area Awards). REGIONAL: Baltimore in Black & White, the cell theatre; Someone Else, NC Stage; The Whole Shebang, Florida Studio Theatre's National Playwrights Festival. TV: "Brainchild," Netflix; "Brain Games," National Geographic (Emmy Award Nominee). UPCOMING: Church & State will have 45 regional productions across 26 states by the end of 2019. The play was also optioned for a movie by Gigi Films. Jason was hired to adapt it into a screenplay with his wife and collaborator Charlotte Cohn. Jason was a winner of the 2012 Hudson Valley Writers Workshop contest and the winner of the 2011 Fixitsolife Theatre playwriting contest. He lives in New York City with his wife, daughter and rescued dog.

CONTACT: jasonodellwilliams@gmail.com

WEBSITE: jasonodellwilliams.com

THE MONOLOGUE

Sara Whitmore:

(Female. 40s. Charlie's wife. A big, brassy, former real estate agent, now stay-at-home mom to their boys MATTHEW (9, athletic and fearless) and LUKE (6, artistic and sensitive). She is sweet, charming and instantly likable. Even when she's bossing you around, she does it with an irresistible smile. More "street smart" than "book smart," but can still hold her own with the big boys. Also born and raised in North Carolina. Loves her family, Jesus and the Bible. She's a tough southern woman with soft underbelly.)

Okay, you wanna make jokes... have your little "mid-life crisis of faith" backstage, be my guest. And we can deal with our marriage after the election. But I will not let you go out in public and belittle something that is important to me! And our sons, and most of this state, just because you lost your temper with some blobber thing-a-ma-gig—

(Charlie tries to interrupt but Sara cuts him off.)

No, no - you had your chance, (with increasing urgency) now let me defend my God who helps me treat people with love and respect, especially those I have a hard time loving, namely you right now, okay?

(Charlie holds up his hands, "okay, sorry, go ahead." Beat.)

Is what happened at our school wrong? Of course it is. It's horrifying and sick and impossible to live with — which is why we need our Faith to help us through.

(Again, Charlie tries to interrupt but Sara cuts him off.)

Uhp! What'd I say?

(He holds his hands up again, "sorry.")

Do we need to do something about guns? (Shrugs.) I don't know. Personally I believe in my right to bear arms, and sure as heck don't want to give up my Baby Glock - but that's not up to me. That's for lawmakers like you to decide. Together. After things cool down. But when you start talkin' all this craziness about there being no God, or prayer is useless… Then you have gone too far, Charlie Whitmore! And I don't know if you snapped or this was a long time comin' or what, but if you keep this up, it is not going to end well. For any of us. So go splash some water on your face, give the speech you always give, and knock off this insanity!

And now, another monologue from Jason Odell Williams.

THE PLAY:

Church & State

SYNOPSIS:

Three days before his bid for reelection, in the wake of a school shooting in his hometown of Raleigh, North Carolina, a Republican U.S. senator makes an off-the-cuff comment to a blogger that gets leaked on "the Twitter," calling into question the senator's stance on guns and God. In this monologue, the senator's liberal Jewish campaign manager, Alex, tries to convince her boss not to go back on the promises he made three days ago during his impromptu speech that shocked the voters and the country and propelled him to a landslide reelection victory.

THE MONOLOGUE:

Alex Klein:

(Female. 30s-40s. Charlie's campaign manager. A fast-talking, no-nonsense liberal Jew from New York whose star is on the rise as a go-to campaign manager. Hired by the Whitmore campaign so she wouldn't defeat him working for the other side. She is great at her job, but knows her career is on the line if this election goes badly. Her self-doubt bubbles to the surface at times, but she's clearly a professional at the top of her game. This monologue comes near the end of the play when Alex is trying to convince the Senator to stick to his new message and be the man she always believed he could be.)

I'm not afraid to admit I made a mistake... (mutters) I just don't make that many of them.

(Charlie tries to interrupt but Alex proceeds with speed and urgency)

But every campaign manager would have done the same thing. With good reason. When you went off-script on Saturday, you stunned that crowd of supporters. This was not the Senator they knew and loved. But eventually they realized you were more interested in principles than towing the party line. And in one of the most Christian, gun-loving states in the nation, the people responded to that with votes! Some voting for the first time in years, voting for your idea: that living without fear is more important than religion or guns or antiquated laws. And yes, I took this job with and eye toward the Oval Office, who wouldn't dream about that? Pictured myself in the West Wing working next to Rob Lowe and Allison Janney.... But none of that matters now - because not only does most of this state believe in you and your new message... But I believe in you. *(Small beat. She becomes a bit emotional.)* Believe you can make a real difference - here and across the country. So no, you can't take back what you said because you're afraid or don't want to work that hard in Washington. You have to stand by what you said, double down on it, and work even harder to prove that you can be the man they voted for! That you are the man they voted for!